A GUIDE TO THE PARABLES

The SPCK International Study Guides incorporate the much loved and respected TEF series, and follow the tradition of: clarity and simplicity; a worldwide, ecumenical perspective; and an emphasis on application of the material studied, drawing out its relevance for Christians today. The Guides are ideal for first year students and Bible study groups, as well as for multi-cultural classes, and students for whom English is a second language.

A NOTE ON TRANSLATIONS OF THE BIBLE

The books of the Bible were originally written in Hebrew, Aramaic and Greek. The best way of understanding what the Bible says is to read it in the original languages. But most of us cannot read Hebrew, Aramaic and Greek. We have to rely on scholars to translate it into our own language. It is almost impossible to translate from one language to another with complete accuracy. Another language, coming from another culture and society, may simply not have the words to express the original experience and understanding. So no translation of the Bible will be perfectly accurate.

For serious study of the Bible, we need a translation which is as close to the original as possible. It is helpful if the translation also reads well in our own language. The English translation of the Bible which the editors of the ISG series recommend for serious study is the *New Revised Standard Version* (NRSV). This translation is very accurate; it is written in clear English, but is not too modern. It is essentially a literal translation which takes into account the latest textual discoveries such as the Dead Sea Scrolls.

The *Revised Standard Version* (RSV), the *New Jerusalem Bible* (NJB) and *New International Version* (NIV) are also suitable for serious study. The Standard edition of the NJB has excellent study aids, but is expensive. The *Good News Bible* reads well, but it is not very accurate. The *Revised English Bible* (REB) updates the New English Bible and combines accuracy with the modern English of daily speech. It is therefore excellent for public and private reading.

You will find it helpful to use a Bible which has cross-references (notes in the margin or at the bottom of the page which point you to other similar passages, or passages from the Old Testament which are quoted in the New Testament).

It is also helpful to have an edition of the Bible which includes the Apocrypha (books such as 1, 2, 3 and 4 Maccabees, Tobit and Ecclesiasticus). These are useful for private reading and study, because they provide important background material for understanding the New Testament, but they are not generally used for public preaching in Protestant churches.

If English is not your home language, compare whatever English translation you use with the Bible translated into your own first language. You may find it helpful to read through each passage in your own language before you study the commentary on the English text.

SPCK International Study Guide 1

A GUIDE TO
THE PARABLES

John Hargreaves

WITH A FOREWORD BY

C. H. Dodd

First published in 1968
SPCK
Holy Trinity Church
Marylebone Road, London NW1 4DU

Revised edition 1979

© John Hargreaves, 1968, 1979

ISBN 0 281 02730 7

11 13 15 17 19 20 18 16 14 12

Printed in Great Britain by
the University Press, Cambridge

Contents

Foreword

There is no part of the Gospels that brings us more directly in touch with the mind of Jesus than the Parables. How natural they are, and how simple! And yet, when you look into them, what depth of meaning! If you have not noticed this before, you certainly will, after reading them again under the guidance of Mr Hargreaves. He lets us see the Parables as what they are, without any forced interpretations: they are living pictures — snapshots sometimes — of the world that Jesus knew in Palestine, with ordinary men and women going about their ordinary affairs — and God is in the middle of it all. Then he shows us how they are also about *us* in *our* ordinary world, and God is there too, offering us His grace and calling us to a decision.

This is a really remarkable little book, soundly based exegetically and ingenious in finding ways of transposing the themes of the Parables into modern situations. Readers who will follow out the method of study that Mr Hargreaves describes so clearly will, I am sure, find that the Parables mean more to them than they have ever meant; but not only so: they will have in their hands a key to the understanding of what the Gospel is about.

C. H. Dodd

Acknowledgements

I should like to thank warmly those very many people who have helped in the preparation of this book; especially:

The Rev. Dr F. W. Dillistone, of Oriel College, Oxford; the Rev. Geraint V. Jones, of Glasgow University; the Rev. Professor C. F. D. Moule, Lady Margaret Professor of Divinity, Cambridge University; and the Rev. David Wilcox, Union Theological College, Bangalore; who generously read and commented on an early version;

The Rev. Roger Tennant, formerly of Korea; and the Rev. Dr Howard Williams of Bloomsbury Baptist Church, London; who by letter and discussion helped me to see better the link between Jesus' parables and life today;

Those Ugandan students whose opinions and questions in the classroom showed me how much more there was in the Parables than I had realized;

Dr John Taylor, General Secretary of the Church Missionary Society, whose encouragement over a long period made possible the completion of this book;

The Community of St Julians, Coolham, Sussex, England who on many occasions provided the best possible surroundings for work;

Miss Daphne Terry, whose lively queries gave much more help and pleasure than one has a right to expect from any editor so that she should really have appeared in this book as co-author; and Miss Jane Robinson who prepared the manuscript so carefully.

JOHN HARGREAVES
Sevenoaks, England

The photographs in this book are reproduced by courtesy of Barnaby's Picture Library (p. 90), Paul Popper Ltd (pp. 77 and 83), and Camera Press Ltd.

The Plan of this book

PART I
A WAY OF STUDYING THE PARABLES

In Part I of this book the author explains the plan which he has used in studying each parable. He also discusses the meaning of the word "parable". It is important therefore to read Part I before beginning the study of the parables in Part II.

PART II
TWELVE PARABLES

It is not possible in a book of this size to study all the parables which are recorded in the Gospels, and so twelve of them have been chosen. By studying and interpreting these twelve we should be able to discover how to interpret the other parables.

Some readers may be interested to notice that these twelve can be divided into four groups:

a. those parables whose chief message seems to be "God has done something new" (numbers 1-3 in this book),

b. those which draw attention to God's love and generosity (numbers 4-7),

c. those which describe the character of the followers of Jesus (numbers 8-10),

d. those which warn us to be ready (numbers 11 and 12).

But although it is useful to notice these four groups, we should not pay *too* much attention to them. First, because we do not know exactly why Jesus told each parable, and secondly because God does not use a parable to say the same thing to each person who hears it.

In addition to the study of these twelve parables, short notes are given on about forty others. The *List of Parables* (pages 131 and 132) shows where notes on these other parables can be found.

Special Notes
Three *Special Notes* are included in Part II. Each of these tries to answer one particular question which people often ask about the parables. These Notes are separate from the chapters about particular parables, partly because of their length, and partly because each concerns more than one parable. But if a reader finds that these Special Notes raise questions that he himself is not asking, then he need not study them further.

Study Suggestions
Suggestions for study appear at the end of each chapter, including the Special Notes. They have been included in order to help a reader who is working alone to study more thoroughly, and also to provide work which a group of students could do together. They are of four kinds:
The *Word Study* suggestions are intended to help a student to check his knowledge of certain key words.
The *Review of Content* is intended to help him check his grasp of the ideas and points of teaching given.
The *Bible Study* suggestions will help him to compare such teaching with teaching found in other parts of the Bible.
The *Opinion and Research* suggestions are intended to help readers to think out the practical applications of the parables to everyday life. These may be especially suitable for use by a group.
Three other points should be noticed:
a. These study suggestions are only *suggestions*. Some readers will not want to use them at all. Other students or a group of students may want to use some of them. Others may want to use them all.
b. The best way to use these suggestions is: *first* to read the parable itself, *secondly* to read the chapter over carefully once or twice, and *lastly* to do the work suggested, in writing, without looking at the chapter except when it is stated that the reader should do so.
c. There is a *Key* at the end of the book so that the reader may check his own work on those questions which can be checked in this way.

Bible Version
The English translation of the Bible used in this book is the *Revised Standard Version* Common Bible Ecumenical Edition (RSV copyright © 1952 and 1971. The *New English Bible* (NEB) is used in cases where it shows the meaning more clearly. See also 'A Note on Translations of the Bible' on p. ii.

Further Reading

Readers may find the following books useful for further study of the Parables; the list includes one or two which present an alternative viewpoint. Some of the older books are now out of print but you should be able to borrow them from a seminary or training centre library or possibly from a friend or colleague.

Kenneth E. Bailey, *Jacob and the Prodigal: How Jesus retold Israel's story*. Bible Reading Fellowship. (Focusing on the Parable of the Prodigal Son.)

John Crossan, *In Parables*. New York and London: Harper & Row.

Bernard Scott, *Hear Then the Parable*. Fortress Press.

V. G. Shillington (ed.), *Jesus and His Parables*. Edinburgh: T. & T. Clark.

David Wenham, *The Parables of Jesus*. London: Hodder & Stoughton.

MORE ADVANCED

Joachim Jeremias, *The Parables of Jesus*. 3rd revised edition. London: SCM Press.

Andrew Parker, *Painfully Clear: The parables of Jesus*. Sheffield Academic Press.

The section on Parables in *The Interpreter's Bible Dictionary* (Nashville: Abingdon Press), *Anchor Bible Dictionary* (New York: Doubleday Image) and Matthew Black and H. H. Rowley (eds), *Peake's Commentary on the Bible* (London: Routledge).

PART I

A WAY OF STUDYING
THE PARABLES

The parables are like bright beams of light. In their light we may see that the living God has a claim on our lives, and make our willing response. They are as simple as that. But if this is so, why does anyone write or read a book about them? Are we like people trying to put sunbeams into a bottle?

Books about parables are written because people ask questions about parables. The author of this present book was recently preaching in a town church on the parable of a Clever Agent in Luke 16. 1-8. After the service two men from the congregation spoke to him about the parable. One said, "I was interested in your interpretation, but how do I know that it is the right interpretation?" The other man said, "I like that parable. But life has changed greatly since the days when Jesus told it. Has it really got a message for us who live today?"

This book tries to answer questions like these. It tries to show that there is a way of approaching the parables which can lead us to discover what God wants us to discover. It tries also to show that, although circumstances have changed, Jesus is teaching us, in His parables, about things that do not change: about ordinary human failures and successes, about our own ordinary fears and hopes, about God's power given to ordinary people.

This introduction suggests a way of studying the parables, which is in three steps.

The first step is reading or hearing the parable.

The second step is trying to discover the original situation, i.e. the situation in which Jesus first told the parable. Along with that goes the teaching which He had in mind, and the teaching which He has for us today.

The third step is to see a parable as a description of our ordinary human lives and our own situations.

I THE FIRST STEP: READING OR HEARING

This means reading the whole parable as we find it in the New Testament, or hearing it read. It also means picturing the whole scene which it describes. We are amused at the humour which it arouses, and

1

we enjoy the surprises which it contains. We do this without asking what teaching it contains: that will come later. We can enjoy it as much as we enjoy any good story which is told round the fire in the evening among friends. Jesus was a wonderful teller of stories, and captured the attention of His listeners.

In this book, each parable is retold in order to make clear certain parts of it. This "retelling" has been called the *Outline*. But reading this Outline should not take the place of reading the story in the Gospels. We need to read carefully the words of the Gospel parable itself at every stage of our study.

II THE SECOND STEP:
SEEING THE ORIGINAL SITUATION

This means finding out, if we can, the circumstances in which Jesus first told the parable, and the special teaching which He wanted His hearers to learn at that time.

1. The circumstances or *situation*. In order to discover this, we ask questions like these:

What was happening in Palestine at that time?

Whom was Jesus speaking to?

Was it to the crowd, or to His disciples, or to His enemies?

What thoughts would His hearers have when they heard this parable?

Who were His enemies and why were they His enemies?

We cannot always answer all these questions when we study a parable, but we can always answer some of them.

Most of the parables were told during a conversation. We must not think of Jesus as a college tutor who has prepared a course of lectures and is going into a classroom. We picture Him, rather, in this way: He is sitting outside someone's house in Jerusalem, taking food with a group of men who have a bad reputation in the city (Luke 15. 1). Some Jewish religious leaders come round the corner. One of them says to his friend, "How can this man Jesus be a good man if he mixes with people of this sort?" Jesus hears, and says, "I heard what you said and I will answer your question. Listen to this story". Then He tells them the parable of the Lost Sheep. If we picture the situation in this way, it becomes clear to us that He told it in order to say this to them: "God's great joy is to forgive and care for people who are in need. My work, therefore, must be to care for such people, even though you despise them." Out of all the great lessons which He could have taught that day, He chose this one. He chose it because he met those people at that time, and this is what they needed to hear.

We have in this way seen the situation in which the parable of the Lost Sheep was told, and we have, as a result, discovered the special teaching which Jesus wanted his hearers to learn from the parable.

2. We are now ready to find out the *application* of a parable to our own lives, i.e. to discover what God wants us to learn from it.

It will help us to do this if we remember the following:

a. A parable was told as a single story. It was the whole story which aroused the feelings of the listeners. They did not think of it as a list of important texts as we are sometimes tempted to do. We, too, should read it as a whole story.

b. There was, as we have seen, one chief message or special teaching.

c. But it would be wrong to think that there is only one lesson in a parable. To some people that parable about the Lost Sheep may be chiefly a warning: to others it will bring comfort. It may bring to us this year something different from the message it brought us some years ago.

d. Yet the message which we find is more likely to be what God wants us to learn if it is in some way connected with the "one chief message".

Some people ask, "Are we not free to take from a parable whatever lesson we find helpful? Is it necessary to find this 'one chief message' which was in the mind of Jesus when he told the story?" The answer is that although this is hard, it *is* necessary. It is the most reliable way of learning what God wants us to learn.

If we simply take from a parable whatever seems to us to be helpful we may indeed receive a true message from God. But we may not. We may, without knowing it, put our own ideas into a parable. If we do this, we find that we become at variance with those who have found quite a different message in it.

e. When we study the parables, we should also study what Jesus taught at other times. Jesus did not teach one thing in His parables, and something different in His other sayings. For example, we have said that the chief lesson Jesus was teaching in the story of the Lost Sheep was that "God's joy is to forgive and care for people in need." We could not have been sure that that was the true teaching if we had not also known other teaching of Jesus with the same message e.g. "It is the sick who need a doctor" (see Mark 2. 17) and "The Son of Man came to seek and to save the lost" (Luke 19. 10).

III THE THIRD STEP:
SEEING OUR OWN SITUATION

This means reading a parable as a description of our own lives, of our own ordinary situations, in which God offers to change and transform us.

In order to do this, it is always wise to return to the parable and read it again. This time we shall notice that Jesus talked about the ordinary happenings of everyday life. He talked about a farmer sowing seed, a woman sweeping the house, workmen being engaged and then complaining about their wages, children playing games, and a tailor mending an old coat. This is the reason why the titles of the chapters of this book refer to "A Tailor", "A Farmer", rather than "The Tailor", "The Farmer", etc.

His parables are not about "religious" people or "religious" services. There are no "religious" people in the parables except for the Pharisee in Luke 18. 10-14, and the Priest and Levite in Luke 10. 30-37. And in these cases their religion was of a mistaken kind. Nor are the parables fables in which tortoises laugh and cats make speeches. Jesus must have known and enjoyed such fables, but He did not use them for His parables.Why? Why did He use the ordinary situations of people's lives?

The answer is because it is in ordinary happenings that we discover who God is and what He is offering us. As we read each parable, each of us can say, "Here is a situation which is like the situations of my own life. It is the happenings of my own life which God offers to fill with new hope. If we don't find God in such things, we shall not find Him anywhere."

Jesus' parables, then, are not just "sermon illustrations" to teach us what God is like. They are not just "earthly stories with heavenly meaning". *They are stories about ordinary life to show what our ordinary lives can become.*

If we read the parables in this way we see that Jesus says special and hopeful things about our lives:

a. The parables describe situations in which *a change is needed.*

A sheep is lost: but that is not the end of the story, for someone exists who can find it. A man finds a treasure in a field: what comes next? What must he do to get the treasure? In these parables (and in most other parables) someone comes to make a change possible — though it is not always accepted.

b. It is *God* who offers a change.

In most of the parables this is not put into words. They do not usually contain the name of God at all. But all the rest of Jesus' teaching shows that this is what He taught. The good news in the parables is that God is at work in the ordinary happenings of our own lives. He knows that we need to be changed in our attitude to these happenings, and He is able to change us.

(We note that He does not offer to take us away from our situations. He offers to change the way in which we behave in these situations. He offers to help us to see them as situations in which we can grow into the kind of people He wants us to become.)

c. It is *our choice* which makes such change possible.

4

In very many of the parables someone has a choice to make. We think of the Prodigal Son choosing to return home, of the Pearl-trader choosing to buy the precious pearl. And whenever Jesus told a parable there were people listening who knew that they must make a choice in their lives *because* they had heard that parable.

NOTE: The difference between Step II and Step III is chiefly a difference between thinking (Step II) and doing and being (Step III). In Step II (Seeing the Original Situation) we are *thinking* of the application to the lives of men and women. But in Step III we go further: we are especially concerned with taking decisions in our own situations, and in other ways with *doing* and *being* what God is calling us to do and be.

CONCLUSION

This, then, is the way in which we shall study the parables which are discussed in this book. Each chapter begins with an *Outline* of the story, and this is our *First Step*. In the *Second* Step we study when and why Jesus originally told the parable. We also think out what lessons it may have for mankind. In our *Third* Step we think of our own situations and what kind of action we can take because we have read this parable. *Finally* some explanatory notes are given on special words or verses in the parable.

STUDY SUGGESTIONS FOR PART I

Word Study

1. Study the words "situation" and "application" as they are used in Part I of this book. For each word, choose *three* of the other words following it in brackets below, which have the same or nearly the same meaning.

   a. Situation (circumstances, post, happenings, promises, events)

   b. Application (request, message, lesson, effect, interpretation)

2. Say in your own words what a parable is.

Review of Content

3. In what way is listening to a parable like listening to any other good story?

4. Why is it important to try to find out the circumstances in which Jesus first told each parable?

5. *a.* Why did Jesus not use "fables"?

   b. Why did He not tell parables about "religious" people?

6. What is the first thing to do when studying a parable?

7. What special teaching did Jesus want His hearers to learn through the parable of the Lost Sheep?

8. Are the following true or untrue? Give reasons for your answer in each case.
   a. When we read a parable we can always tell who Jesus told it to.
   b. We understand a parable best if we read it as a complete story.
   c. A parable never contains more than one single lesson.

Bible Study

9. In what way is the teaching of Romans 5. 8 like the teaching which Jesus gives in the parable of the Lost Sheep?

10. "In His parables Jesus talked about the ordinary happenings of everyday life."
    Which *two* of the following verses show that this is what we should expect Jesus to do?
    John 1. 14;   Phil. 2. 5;   Heb. 4. 15.

Opinion and Research

11. The List of the Parables (on p. 131) shows how many different things Jesus talked about in His parables. How many of these things have you seen in your lifetime?

12. a. Write down two things that you often do, which nobody could have done who was living in Palestine at the same time as Jesus.
    b. Since life has changed so much, can a parable that was told at that time have a message for us today? Give reasons for your answer.

13. This chapter refers to stories about changes that are needed. In each case the change becomes possible because one person makes a choice. Write a brief story of the same kind.

14. "If we don't find God in the ordinary happenings of our own lives, we shall not find Him anywhere."
    Do you agree? Give reasons for your answer.

PART II

TWELVE PARABLES
WITH THREE SPECIAL NOTES

Chapter 1.   A Tailor and an Old Coat

Mark 2. 21; Matt. 9. 16; Luke 5. 36
The Parable of the Patched Garment

I   OUTLINE

The saying of Jesus as it is found in Mark 2. 21 reads: "No one sews a piece of unshrunk cloth on an old garment; if he does, the patch tears away from it, the new from the old, and a worse tear is made."

If we were to put this little parable into the form of a story it might be something like this:

A man was looking at his old coat, noticing the places where it was badly torn. He remembered that he had a piece of newly-woven cloth in the house, so he took this piece of cloth and his old coat to the tailor. But the tailor said, "I can't patch your old coat with that cloth. No one puts new cloth that has not been cleaned (or shrunk) on old cloth. If I did that and you wore it in the rain, the new piece would shrink and the holes would be bigger than ever." (Then perhaps the tailor added, "You need a new coat.")

II   SEEING THE ORIGINAL SITUATION

The situation
Some people came to Jesus with a problem. They said, "The Pharisees are fasting. Why are your disciples not fasting?" In His answer Jesus did not lay down a rule about fasting. He used their question to tell them about Himself.

First He told them a little parable about the Wedding Guests not Fasting. By Jewish custom they were excused from fasting because the wedding was a time of joy (Mark 2. 19, 20). By this parable He was saying, "This is a time of joy for my disciples, because something new has happened in the world. God has begun to rule over mankind in a new way." This is the meaning of Mark 1. 15 (NEB): "The time has come; the Kingdom of God is upon you," and according to Matthew 12. 28 He added that they would see that this was so if they watched what He did and listened to what He said.

In order to make this clear Jesus then told two more short parables. This one that we are studying, about an old coat, is the first of them. The other one says, "You cannot put new wine into old skins" (Mark 2. 22).

The chief message of the parable, therefore, is this:

"*It is not enough just to patch up the old religion of the Jews or to add one or two new customs to it. Do not try to mix the old way and the new way which I have come to bring.*"

Suggested Application

Jesus Christ, by His coming and living and dying and rising, has made possible new ways of living. This parable begs us not to confuse them with the old ways. The life which Jesus made possible was new in the following ways:

1. We now have a new reason for *believing* in God. People believed because they had seen Jesus. Anyone who saw Jesus was seeing God. "Anyone who has seen Me has seen the Father" (John 14. 9, NEB). This parable says, "Notice that this is new teaching. It is something more than just putting a patch on what people thought about God before Jesus came."

2. We have been given a new reason for *hoping*. Jesus had victory over evil in all that He did: in the miracles that He did, and in His rising out of the grave alive. This was the beginning of the victory that God will have over all evil in the end. Now we are sure that God cannot be defeated. That is why Christians are people with hope.

3. We have been given a new reason for *believing that we are accepted* by God. Under the old way (among the Jews) men tried to make themselves acceptable to God by keeping the law of Moses. But the coming of Jesus has shown that people never do keep it, and that, in spite of this, God will accept them. We are therefore accepted by God *in spite of* our failures, not *because* of our successful living. We are accepted by God because of His generosity and "grace", because He forgives us although we do not deserve it.

Those who believe this are joined to God by a "new covenant", which takes the place of the old covenant made by God with Moses and others. (In the Bible, "covenant" is an agreement which binds God and man together. It shows that God does not abandon man, and reminds man that he belongs to God.) Paul tells us that Jesus said at the Last Supper, "This cup is the *new* covenant" (1 Cor. 11. 25). They are living "in the new life of the Spirit", no longer "under the old written code" (Rom. 7. 6).

Christians are never free from the temptation to serve God in the old ways, e.g. to try to win His approval by doing good. We are tempted

8

to think that going to church and reading the Bible and contributing to Church funds and keeping the laws of the country are the whole of Jesus' religion. But when we think like this we are going back to the old ways.

III   SEEING OUR OWN SITUATION

The parable shows us a poor man looking at his old coat and saying, "This coat cannot be mended. What shall I do? Can I get a new one?"

We know that in our own lives it is often painful to give up an old thing or an old custom. We sometimes avoid the new thing by trying to patch the old one. Here are some examples showing how God offers us new ways. We shall see in each case that someone had to take a decision: to accept the new way, or try to patch the old. We shall see that we are here concerned with what we *do*, not only with what we *think*.

1. Here is a farmer who learns of a new way of farming which seems good to him. He accepts it and the cost which it involves and leaves the old way. He is a Christian, and has learnt that God is concerned with the growing of food and that He offers us new ways of doing it.

(Perhaps it should be added here, that of course not all new ways are good ways. What we are saying is that whenever any person or any congregation believes that a new way is God's gift to them, then this gift must not be refused through fear, nor should it be used to patch up the old way.)

2. Here is a parent who, while travelling about his country, sees that some customary ways of treating children are no longer right. He is a Christian, and as soon as he returns home to his wife, they begin to think out together new ways of bringing up their children.

They see that if they adopt new ways, they will not be saying that the old ways were bad. They will be thanking God that He has shown them new ways that are better. The new ways will now have to take the place of the old.

3. Here is a man who is not a Christian. Now he has met a true Christian and asks to be baptized. He sees that if he becomes a Christian his life will have to turn round and face a new way. And he sees that he will have to leave his old ways of living.

Very soon the temptation comes to him to keep some of his old ways and to mix with them the new life of being a Christian. He is tempted to put away some of the old bad habits but to keep others. He is tempted to keep the regulations of the Church but to live in a spirit and manner which belonged to his old life. So he is being tempted to put a "patch" on his old life. He becomes "torn" and "divided" like a coat which is badly patched. He has no joy in his new life.

9

'Jesus Christ has made possible new ways of living . . . in our own lives it is often painful to give up an old thing or an old custom' (pp. 8–9).

In this Malaysian store a customer has decided that he must replace his old jacket with a new one, and is willing to pay the cost.

God offers him a life that is new in all its parts. If he accepts it, he can serve God with the whole of his life and the whole of himself. NOTE: This does not, of course, mean that when we become Christians we must give up all the things which we did before. A man who worked in a newspaper office became a Christian and said to a friend, "I shall have to leave this office now. There is so much dishonesty here. I would like to be trained as a preacher." But his friend said, "No. You should stay in your office and serve God there. You can be honest there, even though some others are not." What we have to give up is usually not the things we do but the way in which we do them. St Paul says, "You must be made new in mind and spirit" (Eph. 4. 23, NEB. See also 2 Cor. 5. 17.)

4. Here is a group of Christians who have begun to believe that it is sinful to remain separated from other Christians in the same country. They meet with Christians of other denominations and worship with them. They think together of ways in which their Churches can become fully united. They see that if they become one Church there will be many changes. Some of the old ways are still good and can be brought into a United Church, but many other customs will now have to be given up.

South India is one place where this happened. After thirty years of preparation the Christians had to decide if they would put away old divisions and become one Church. In 1947 they decided to do this. It was painful to lose some of the old customs they knew: many of them were fearful about the future. But the new way offered by God was accepted.

5. Here is a congregation which is thinking about the best ways in which God can be worshipped when Christians come together. They believe that many of the old ways were suitable for the old days but are no longer suitable. But can they find new ways which use the music of today and the words of today?

NOTES

a. **Short parables and long parables.** Some readers divide the parables of Jesus into three kinds:

a. Full-length story-parables, such as the parable of the Good Samaritan.

b. Long sayings, such as the one studied in this chapter.

c. Short sayings. These are the shortest parables of all, e.g. "Can a blind man lead a blind man?"

There is no difference between these three kinds except their length. There is a story in all of them. In the case of the first group it is told in full; in the case of the sayings it is not told, but only referred to.

11

b. Parables with the same teaching. We may notice here three other short parables in which Jesus seems to be saying the same thing that He taught in the parable of a Tailor and an Old Coat:
1. A Kingdom Split in Two, and
2. A Strong Man Overcome (Mark 3. 23-27).

In these two parables Jesus was saying: "You have seen the things that I do. You can see that the powers of evil are now being divided and destroyed. A new thing is taking place."
3. A Fig-Tree with New Shoots (Mark 13. 28).

As far as we can tell, Jesus taught this: "Summer has come and the trees have new life. Do not live as if it were still winter."

c. Garment. We have called it a "coat" in this chapter because there is no other word in English to describe the kind of garment that Jesus was talking about. It was worn over other clothes. In the Authorized Version it is called a "cloak".

STUDY SUGGESTIONS FOR CHAPTER I

Word Study

1. Two important words are used in this chapter, "grace" and "covenant". Which *two* of the phrases following it in brackets help to show the meaning of each of these words?
Grace is (a kind of generosity) (a reward for good people) (given in spite of sin).
Covenant is (a law given to the Israelites) (a kind of agreement) (a reminder that we belong to God).

2. The parable we have studied is about an outer garment or "coat". Compare this word with the translation of it given in:
a. another English version;
b. any other language you know.

Review of Content

3. What parable comes immediately after this parable of a Tailor and an Old Coat? Say whether its teaching is the same or different, and in what way.

4. Why did Jesus tell the story of Wedding Guests not Fasting (Mark 2. 19, 20)?

5. What special teaching did Jesus want His listeners to learn through the parable of a Tailor?

6. "Jesus has made possible new ways of living." What are two of these new ways, in your opinion?

12

7. Are the following true or untrue? Give reasons for your answer in each case.
   a. All new ways are good ways.
   b. If parents adopt new ways of bringing up their children, it shows that they think all old ways are bad.
   c. When we become Christians we must give up all the things we did before.

8. Read Mark 2. 21 again. Then retell this parable in the form of a story.

Bible Study

9. Read Mark 2. 21; Matt. 9. 16; and Luke 5. 36.
   a. What phrase is used in Mark which is not used in the other verses?
   b. In what way is Luke's verse different from the other two?

10. In what way is the teaching of Mark 3. 27 like the teaching of the parable of a Tailor?

11. a. Which two of the following passages are "full-length story-parables?"
    b. Which two are "long sayings"?
    c. Which two are "short sayings"?
    Matt. 11. 16, 17; 13. 3-8; 13. 24-30; 13. 33; 15. 11; 19. 24.

Opinion and Research

12. a. Do you think that Christians are really more ready than other people to accept new ways, e.g. in farming, cooking, etc?
    b. Ought they to be more ready?
    c. If they are not, why do you think they are not?

13. "We are never free from the temptation to serve God in the old way." An example of this is given in the chapter. Give another example from everyday life.

14. Do you think that we should use the music of today and the language of today in our Church services? Give reasons for your answer.

15. Find out which Church regulations of your own Church, or of some other Church, have been changed during the last twenty-five years, e.g. concerning marriage or other important matters. Say where you obtained your information in each case.

16. What would you reply to someone who said: "I agree that trouble comes when we try to mix old ways with new ways. Why should I not keep to the old?"

Chapter 2.   A Farmer and his Seeds

Mark 4. 26-29
The Parable of the Seed Growing of Itself

I OUTLINE

This is not really a story, but a description of what every farmer did in the land where Jesus lived.
He dug the ground and sowed his seed. When that was done, there was nothing more that he could do. So he turned his attention to all the other jobs which must be done on a farm: he fed his cattle, and mended his tools, and repaired his house. When each day came to an end he slept well, knowing that his seed was growing. Each morning when he got up he saw that the growing was continuing. Each week he noticed the stages of this growing: one week he saw a green blade appear, like a blade of grass, another week the ear appeared, which would ripen and give him food. But how all this growth took place was not an anxiety for him. He weeded the ground to let the rain reach the new plant, but the growing took place without his help. It even reached harvest without his help. What he did was to harvest it.

II SEEING THE ORIGINAL SITUATION

The situation
This parable was probably told during the first year of the teaching ministry of Jesus. His work had begun, but there were difficulties. Many Jewish religious leaders were against Him. Some of the ordinary people only followed Him because they hoped He would do miracles for them. Even the disciples must have been sometimes disappointed. Jesus had told them that God had begun to rule in a new way ("The time is fulfilled, and the Kingdom of God is at hand; repent, and believe in the gospel," (Mark 1. 15), but it sometimes seemed doubtful if this was true. And it must have been hard to believe that God would one day rule over all mankind.

The disciples may have become as impatient as some of the people. At that time there were in Palestine movements of nationalist Jews against the Roman colonial government (see Acts 5. 36, 37). Some of these people believed that they must openly proclaim God as their ruler and king and that they could only do this if they threw off the authority of the Roman Emperor. One of the disciples, Simon, belonged to a group like this, called the Zealots.

It is probable that even Jesus was tempted to be impatient and to make people accept God as their King by force. This seems likely from

St Luke's story of His temptations in chapter 4. 1-13.

It was probably in this kind of situation that Jesus told the parable of a Farmer and his Seeds. Here is its chief message:

"The seed has now been sown, that is, God has truly began to rule. He really is at work among people in a new way, although you find it hard to believe this.

The result is in His hands, not in yours. Seeds grow of themselves: farmers do not push them up."

Suggested Application

1. Because a Christian has confidence in God, he learns how to control anxiety.

We can rely on God completely because He has a plan for the world and for ourselves. And He has the power to put His plan into effect. It will not be defeated by any event that could happen. It will not be defeated even when all life on earth comes to an end.

Jesus showed that He had this confidence by the way in which He lived. He did not only say frequently, "Do not be anxious" (see Matt. 6. 25, 28, 31, 34); He did His whole work without worrying, even in the days just before His own death. His confidence in God was two-fold. He had confidence that God was in control in present events, and also that God would be in control when life on this earth comes to an end.

We are today greatly tempted to be anxious and to despair as we see what is happening. We see Christian workers being expelled from a country. We see an increasing number of married people being divorced. We see wars being fought in many parts of the world. We are tempted to despair, and to say, "Can God ever rule over mankind?"

The farmer in the parable slept well at night: when we cannot sleep at night, the reason sometimes is that we have not sufficient confidence in God.

2. Because a Christian has confidence in God, he learns how to overcome impatience.

Jesus was wonderfully patient and unhurried, as He did His work. He had only a short time in which to do it, yet He did not rush about. He clearly believed that God was the One who was in control. He said calmly, "My Father has never yet ceased His work, and I am working too" (John 5. 17, NEB). This is the reason why He spent so much time in prayer. It is also the reason why He was content to visit "unimportant" people as well as the religious leaders.

Impatience and "rushing about" and over-work are the special temptations of many highly educated people today. We look at rich men and say, "They made their money by working"; we look at scientists who send space-probes to circle other planets and we say, "They did it through hard work." So we think *all* important problems

15

can be solved by working harder and by sleeping less. But this is not so. A husband and wife do not learn to live together in love by rushing about and working till late at night. A guilty person does not find the peace of God's forgiveness by more work. In such matters the important thing is to know when to work hard but also to know when to stop working. There was a Nigerian lorry on which was written, "Let go, let God." This saying, if rightly interpreted, sums up the teaching of this parable.

3. A Christian provides opportunities for growth.

We have seen that the parable does not encourage us to be lazy. Lazy farmers are unsuccessful farmers. It shows us that the farmer prepared the ground for the seeds; he provided opportunities for the growing to take place; he sowed the seed and kept the ground weeded (see v. 26). In these days, of course, there is much else that a farmer can do, e.g. by rotation of crops, using fertilizers and weed-killers, etc.

We are to make opportunities through which God will do His work. We must make opportunities for others and for ourselves.

This is what we do when we urge the government to build enough houses for those who live in a town. The houses will not make people good. But when people are crowded together into unclean little rooms, it is very difficult indeed for them to hear what God says to them.

This is what doctors do when they vaccinate people or perform an operation. They help a man's body to resist disease, or to heal up "of itself". It is God, not the doctor, who actually heals.

This is what a hard-working pastor does. His work is to make opportunities for God to work among the people: he does this by meeting them, listening to them, talking with them, and praying for them. When he has done this, he has done his best, and he commits the people to God and is not anxious.

III SEEING OUR OWN SITUATION

Let us go back to the parable. We are very often in situations which are like the situation of that farmer. We have worked hard in some matter. The important question now is, "Do we trust God to look after the results?" We have a choice between trusting and worrying. If we trust Him, we can begin to face our situation in a new way. This happens so often that we need only a few examples:

The parents of a girl have done their best to bring her up well. Now she has left school and has gone to work in another town. Her parents have to make a choice. *Either* they worry about her, *or* they say, "We have done our best. We shall go on doing our best for her by writing to her regularly and praying for her. But God has her in His hands. We have confidence in God, so we have confidence in her too."

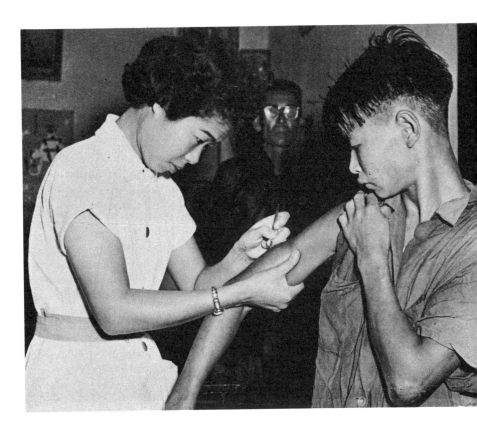

"We are to make opportunities through which God will do His work . . The result of our work is in His hand."

This vaccinator belongs to the Hong Kong "flying doctor" team which serves isolated villages. She is creating an opportunity for the boy's body to become resistant to a particular disease.

Two people have quarrelled bitterly. The first one tells the other that he is sincerely sorry for his share in the quarrel, and asks for forgiveness. But the other refuses. The first one *either* goes on worrying about the quarrel, *or* he commits the matter to God. If he can leave the matter in God's hands, there is peace for him. He can turn his attention to his work with his whole heart. (See Luke 10. 6.)

A Welfare Officer in a factory is doing his best to bring peace between two groups of workers who disagree strongly about wages. He has done what he can, but he is not sure if they will accept his advice. *Either* he will worry (and probably become angry) because there is doubt if they will listen to him, *or* he will commit the matter to God, firmly believing that God is at work among all the people of that factory.

A schoolboy has heard teaching about following Jesus Christ. He is not a Christian, but he wants to be a Christian. Yet he does not know if he really is willing to follow Jesus or not. He begins to worry. Then someone shows him the verse, "My grace is sufficient for you" (2 Cor. 12. 9). He sees that he will *either* go on worrying and thinking, *or* he will accept the things that God has done for him already and commit himself with all his faults and all his unanswered questions into God's hands.

Once again we notice that in Step III we are chiefly concerned with doing and being (i.e. actively trusting God), as the result of reading this parable. The *thinking* of Step II was a preparation for this.

NOTES

a. Seed upon the ground (v. 26). We have seen that the chief message of this parable is that God is at work among people just as He is at work in the ground when seeds have been sown.

It is important to notice that the "ground" in which God is at work is not just the Church. Jesus does not say this anywhere in the Gospels. The "ground" is the world, and God is at work among *all* people. This is what Paul taught when he said in Acts 14.17 that God "did not leave himself without witness". When we understand this, we really can commit all things into His hands.

b. The seed should sprout and grow, he knows not how (v. 27). People who read this today sometimes say, "In those days farmers did not know how seeds become plants, but we do know." It is true that we know more than the farmer in the parable about the way in which plants grow: that they grow by taking in carbon dioxide from the air, and by feeding on nutrients which come through the moisture which is in the soil, and by taking in light from the sun, and so on. But we do not know everything, even today. We do not yet know what the power is which is the "life" of the seed.

However, we do not believe in God chiefly because we have not yet discovered what "life" is. We do not believe in God chiefly because He fills up the empty spaces in our knowledge. God is not just the word we use when we do not know the reason for something that happens.

People who believe in God chiefly because He fills up spaces in our knowledge find it harder to believe in Him each time a new discovery is made. They feel that He is being pushed further and further away.

God is our God because He is the giver of all power and all knowledge. Scientists make discoveries because God has made them able to do so. If one day they discover how to make "life", the discovery will be the result of God's Spirit in man.

c. The earth produces of itself (v. 28). These are the important words of the parable. The Greek word which is translated "of itself" is *automatike*.

These words are sometimes translated "The earth produces secretly", and the parable has sometimes been called the parable of the "Seed Growing Secretly". But this is not the meaning.

It is important to give correct titles to parables. Some of the people who translated the Bible into English thought it would help readers if each page had a title to show what it contained. So they invented titles for the parables according to their own interpretation of them. But sometimes their interpretation was a mistaken one, and this has led readers to give a wrong interpretation too.

d. First the blade, then the ear (v. 28b). These words only describe a plant which is growing. It does not mean that God rules over more and more people every year, or that human beings are gradually getting better and better. Jesus did not teach that. We do not see it happening.

e. The harvest has come (v. 29). Some of those who interpret this parable say that these are the important words. Their interpretation is as follows:

The seed in the parable is the word of God which was sown in the world before the coming of Jesus. The coming of Jesus was the harvest. The work of the disciples was to join Jesus in reaping the harvest, that is, in bringing people to accept God as their king. This interpretation is supported by Luke 10. 2, "The harvest is plentiful, but the labourers are few", and by John 4. 35-38.

There is a difference between this interpretation and the one which is given in this chapter. But both agree in saying that "the success of God's work lies in *His* hands."

19

STUDY SUGGESTIONS FOR CHAPTER 2

Word Study

1. A Christian "has confidence in" God. Choose *five* out of the following words or phrases which have the same meaning or nearly the same meaning:

   relies on   speaks to   believes in
   has faith in   needs   trusts
   associates with   commits himself to

2. What did a "Zealot" want to do?

3. The Greek word *automatike* in Mark 4. 28a is translated "of itself" (RSV). Compare this with the translation of it given in:
   a. another English version;
   b. any other language you know.

Review of Content

4. The parable of a Farmer and his Seeds does not encourage a farmer to be lazy. Give a list of seven words which are used in the Outline to show what a farmer of those days had to do.

5. What special teaching did Jesus want His hearers to learn through the parable of a Farmer and his Seeds?

6. Are the following true or untrue? Give reasons for your answer in each case.
   a. Good houses make good people.
   b. Doctors can help a man's body to resist disease or heal up after an injury as God intends it to do.

7. Why is it misleading to call Mark 4. 26-29 "the parable of the Seed Growing Secretly"?

Bible Study

8. This chapter contains the following statements. Find verses from John chapters 5 and 6 which support them.
   a. Many Jewish religious leaders were against Jesus.
   b. Some of the ordinary people only followed Jesus because they hoped He would do miracles for them.
   c. Even the disciples must have been sometimes disappointed.

9. "Jesus was content to meet unimportant people."
   Give two examples of such people from Matthew chapter 8.

10. *a.* Which one of the following Psalms expresses a truth which is most like the teaching of the parable of a Farmer and his Seeds? Psalm 6; Psalm 46; Psalm 130.
    b. Which verse of that Psalm expresses this teaching most clearly?

11. What teaching contained in Luke 10. 6 is also contained in this parable?

Opinion and Research

12. The chapter contains examples of precious things which cannot be obtained simply by working harder. Give another example.

13. We read in this chapter of a girl who left home. What difference would it make to her if her parents trusted God and trusted their daughter?

14. Farmers of today can do more to help their crops grow than the farmers of the old days. Suggest two things a farmer of today can do that a farmer of Jesus' time could not. Say where you obtained your information.

15. *a.* Why is it important to say that the "ground" in which God is at work is the world and is not just the Church?
    b. What difference would you notice in the work and behaviour of someone who really believed this?

16. "I believe in God chiefly because He fills up the empty spaces in our knowledge."
    Why is belief of this kind unsatisfactory?

Chapter 3. A Farmer and his Harvest

Mark 4. 1-8; Matt. 13. 1-8; Luke 8. 4-8
The Parable of the Sower

I OUTLINE

A farmer began his sowing. He sowed his seed wherever there was any hope that it might grow. He sowed on ground which people had begun to make into a pathway, on rocky ground, and on ground that was full of thorn-bushes. He sowed also, of course, on the best ground. He sowed everywhere because, like all farmers in that part of the world, he used to plough his land after sowing it. It was his custom to plough up the whole land, the part that had been trodden down as well as the part that had thorn-bushes on it, the poor soil as well as the rich soil.

But on this occasion the birds took away some of the seed he had sowed on the path before he could do the ploughing; the sun burnt up the new shoots on the rocky ground; and the thorn-bushes had already begun to spoil more of the crop.

In spite of this, however, harvest time showed that his work had not been wasted. As he looked at the harvest from the whole of his land, he saw that it was a big harvest, perhaps bigger than his neighbours expected.

II SEEING THE ORIGINAL SITUATION

The situation

This is another of the parables which Jesus seems to have told during the first year of His teaching ministry. It was a time of difficulty and disappointment for His disciples. See page 14, lines 20-37. Jesus was the greatest and best person they had ever known, and yet they saw that He was being regarded as an enemy by their own religious leaders. He was accused of "blasphemy" (Mark 2. 7), of madness (Mark 3. 21), and of sorcery (Mark 3. 22). Very few people had any faith in Him (Mark 6. 5, 6), and some even drove Him away (Luke 4. 29). His followers must often have asked the question, "Is Jesus' work really going to be successful? He says that God began to rule in a new way when He Himself began His Ministry. But can God succeed if Jesus fails?"

It is not possible to say what Jesus Himself was thinking. But we know that He had His own temptations. Was He tempted to doubt if His work would succeed? If He was, then this parable shows that He overcame the temptation.

The chief message that Jesus was giving in this parable was this:

22

"Although the power of evil is strong, God is stronger and He will not fail to rule over mankind."
It will be seen that the message of this parable is like the message of the parable of a Farmer and his Seeds (chapter 2). In that parable Jesus was saying, "The result of God's rule over man is in His hands. Don't be anxious." In this parable He said, "The success of God's work is certain. So don't be downhearted or surprised when you see that evil is strong."
NOTE: In this chapter we are paying special attention to the parable itself (vv. 3-8); but the interpretation given above is an interpretation of the whole passage and not only of verses 3-8. See Note c. below for a comment on verses 13-20.

Suggested Application
There are two great truths contained in this parable: 1. The truth that evil is strong; 2. The truth that God's power is stronger.
1. The farmer knew that his work in some parts of the farm would be wasted. But he was accustomed to that. Birds, rocks, and thorns were well-known enemies of the farmer and his seeds. So in spite of all these things, he did his sowing.
The interpretation in vv. 13-20 draws attention to "the enemies", that is, the evil in the world. See especially vv. 15-19.
So Christians are being taught to accept the fact that there is sin and evil in the world. They must learn that much of their life and work may be wasted. They will see that some of this waste is due to sin, either their own or other people's (e.g. when a child is killed through the carelessness of a car-driver). Some of the waste, however, they will not be able to understand at all and they will find it hard to see why God has allowed it (e.g. when a great leader, on whom many people are depending, is drowned in a flood). They live and work in the name of God, they do their best to love and serve other people, but they must not be surprised when people refuse to take notice of God, or when they reject their love and help, or when disasters occur.
2. But the farmer had a big harvest in spite of all his wasted work. So we Christians are made sure by this parable that God's plan for the world will succeed. Those who follow Jesus and put themselves under God as their King are taking part in a battle against evil which God will win.
If we accept these two truths we are saved from despair. Despair comes to us when we do not look straight at evil, and are surprised when it comes. One Christian congregation had a very fine leader whose character was almost like the character of Christ. But very many people in that town refused to listen to what he said. Unjust accusations were made against him. Some laughed at the good things he was doing.

A member of that congregation, seeing how he was being treated, found it hard to believe in God's power and goodness. He said, "Does this man's life not please God? Why is he being persecuted?" Yet there was nothing surprising about the persecution. Jesus Himself was killed.

Despair also comes to us when we forget that God cannot be defeated.

A grown-up Christian, then, says something like this: "Sin is like a disease throughout the world. It is in others and it is in me. Because of it, disaster and pain and waste come for others and for me and for God's Church. But God has come to earth and has begun to rule over mankind in a new way. He is ruling now and one day His rule over mankind will be complete."

"Christians learn that much of their life and work may be wasted . . . Some of the waste they will not be able to understand at all. But God's plan for the world will succeed. If we accept these two truths we are saved from despair."

Some years ago more than 300 people died and 10,000 houses were destroyed in an earthquake in Sicily. Many people must have felt, like this man, that life was finished.

24

III SEEING OUR OWN SITUATION

Seeing the world around us
As we look at the world we see waste and loss and pain and failure:

A good father dies, broken-hearted because his son has not written nor been to see him for ten years, and believing that his love for the son was wasted.

A girl loses her job in an office because she refuses to share in the dishonest practices of the others. She cannot find other work.

A country sends food to another country where there is great hunger. But the food goes into the "black market", and never reaches the hungry people.

The Church in one country sends many good Christians to try to build a strong Church in another country. But after 100 years the Church there is still only a handful of people.

When we hear about such things or when we see such things happening, what do we do? We *either* despair *or* we learn the lesson of this parable. We have this choice, for instance, every time we listen to the radio news or read a newspaper.

What difference will it make to us if we choose to follow Jesus' teaching in this parable?

First, we shall be led to look at God with faith, and to say, "Those four stories are not yet finished. God is not going to be defeated in those places. He is not only at work in the soil, but He is at work in people's homes and offices and churches."

Secondly, even if the love of that father, for instance, did not do what he hoped it would do, that love was not wasted. The father, by loving, was joining himself with God and His loving. This is what gives value to our lives — to work alongside God.

Thirdly, we shall make our faith in God result in action. A group of Christians helped the young people in their town to open a club. The young people twice destroyed the building. Now that Christian group is trying again to help the same young people, although this time they might do it in a different way.

Seeing ourselves
As we look at ourselves, we have the same choice to make: we *either* despair *or* we have faith in God's power to overcome what is evil in the world and in ourselves.

If we are honest, we shall find enough to make us despair. We look at the ways in which we have wasted God's gifts and the opportunities He has given us: we look at our own selfishness. But a mature Christian knows what to do when he is tempted to despair.

The farmer did not stop sowing because of the thorns and the sun

25

and the rock. If we choose to follow the teaching of the parable, there are several things we can do. First, we can try to know ourselves. This means knowing both our strength and our special weaknesses and temptations. We can do this through examining ourselves, and also through allowing someone else (perhaps our wife or husband) to tell us what we are like. When we know our own weaknesses they do not become less serious, but they surprise us less. Then we accept God's offer to start again after a failure or a disaster. We can start again because we believe He is at work in us just as He is at work in the soil in our garden.

NOTES

a. Other Parables. As far as we can see, Jesus told many parables during the first part of His ministry and made the same great declaration in them all. This declaration was, "God's rule has begun. Take courage!"

This parable of a Farmer and His Harvest is one of these. So also are the parables which we studied in chapters 1 and 2.

There are other parables which Jesus probably told at the same time:

Wedding Guests not Fasting (Mark 2. 19, 20), in which Jesus was saying: "This is a time of *joy* because God is in control."

A Woman and her Yeast (Luke 13. 21; Matt. 13. 33), in which He was saying: "God is ruling now in a new way, and there will be great *changes* in the world."

Children at Play (Luke 7. 31-35; Matt. 11. 16-19): "A great thing has happened. Are you going to take no *notice* of it?"

The Mustard Seed (Mark 4. 30-32; Luke 13. 18, 19; Matt. 13. 31, 32): "The new Kingdom of God is for *all* people."

Weeds in the Wheat (Matt. 13. 24-30) and the Fisherman's Net (Matt. 13. 47, 48), in which the chief teaching seems to be: "God, as He rules, will divide true followers from false. It is *not your* work to divide them. Do not be anxious about those who refuse to listen to Jesus."

b. Mark 4, 10-12. These verses are not part of the parable. They describe a conversation between Jesus and His followers. At first sight Jesus seems to have been saying in these verses that He did not want certain people to understand His parables. But these points should be noticed:

1. Verse 12 is quoted from Isaiah 6. 9, 10.

2. According to St Matthew, Jesus said that He used parables *"because,* hearing, they do not understand" (Matt. 13. 13). This is quite different from what St Mark says: *"so that* they may hear but not understand" (Mark 4. 12).

"As we look at the world we see waste and loss and pain and failure."
But the Sicilians rebuilt their towns, and children made homeless by the earthquake have grown up to live their own lives, and, themselves bear children.

3. Many people therefore think that Matthew has understood Jesus' words better than St Mark did. They say that Mark thought that Jesus did not want the Jews to understand His message until the non-Jews (the Gentiles) could also share it. (This is like the words of St Paul in Rom. 11. 25.)

4. Jesus did want people to understand His parables. He told parables to interest them, to make them think, to make them take a decision about Himself (to follow Him or not to follow Him). He told parables so that they might change their way of living.

5. Perhaps the words of Jesus mean this: "When I teach, some people understand and some do not. My parables and all my teaching divide people. This is what happened in the days of Isaiah. You remember what he wrote about those who did not listen."

c. Verses 13-20. In these verses we are given an interpretation of the parable. If we read them as part of the parable itself, they are hard to understand. They are hard for two reasons.

1. The first reason is because in vv. 1-8 attention is chiefly on the sower and on his successful harvest, but in vv. 13-20 attention is on the different kinds of soil. There is no disagreement between the two passages, but they do not quite fit.

2. The second reason is that they seem to turn the parable into an allegory. In an allegory there are several different parts in a story and each part has its own different piece of teaching in it. In this case there are four kinds of soil and each kind of soil is compared to one kind of person to whom the teaching of Jesus comes.

Jesus may have used allegories. We cannot say that He did not do so; but allegories are longer than parables and are therefore more often written down. We know that Jesus' parables were spoken, not written. See Special Note B, on Parables and Allegories, p. 67.

For these (and other) reasons many people who have studied the matter carefully believe that vv. 13-20 are an interpretation of the parable which Christian leaders made afterwards. They remind us that preachers interpreted the parables in order to apply them to the needs of their congregations, as a preacher today preaches a sermon based on a parable of Jesus. If this is so, then we shall regard vv. 13-20 as providing something true and valuable which arises out of the parable, not as saying anything contrary to it. See Special Note A, p. 31.

In this chapter we have the whole passage in mind: vv. 1-20.

STUDY SUGGESTIONS FOR CHAPTER 3

Word Study

1. What do the following words mean: "blasphemy", "sorcery"?

2. The word "despair" is much used in this chapter. Which three words out of the following mean the *opposite* (or nearly the opposite) of despair?

   hope   fear   trust   faith   waste

Review of Content

3. Why were Jesus' disciples sometimes disheartened?

4. Some people think that Mark 4. 13-20 is the interpretation of the parable which Christians made afterwards and not Jesus' own interpretation. What reasons are there for thinking this?

5. What special teaching did Jesus want His hearers to learn through:
   a. The parable of Children at Play (Luke 7. 31-35)?
   b. The parable of Wedding Guests not Fasting (Mark 2. 19, 20)?

6. What is the chief difference between Matt. 13. 13 and Mark 4. 12?

7. Did Jesus want His parables to be understood by His disciples only, or by other people also?

8. "A mature Christian is one who has learnt what to do when he is tempted to despair" (p. 25).
   What two things can we do when we are tempted to despair?

Bible Study

9. "Christians take part in a battle against evil which God will win" (p. 25). Which verse in Relevation 19. 1-8 supports this statement?

10. For each of the following passages choose a parable from the list on p. 26 which contains similar teaching.
    a. Isaiah 43. 18, 19; b. Rev. 7. 9.

11. In what way is the teaching of Ecclesiastes 11. 4 like the teaching of the parable of a Farmer and his Harvest?

Opinion and Research

12. a. Read a recent copy of a newspaper and write down all the headlines of articles which report war, crime, pain, and suffering.
    b. Which of the parables mentioned in this chapter gives you most help in reading that newspaper without despair?

13. During a discussion on evil spirits and witchcraft, someone said, "A Christian should not believe that such powers exist." Do you agree? What is the message of this parable on the subject?

29

14. Birds, rocks, and thorns prevented the seeds from growing fully.
    a. Suggest three other things which may spoil a harvest today.
    b. If the parable were rewritten so that it told the story of a father and his growing children instead of a farmer and his seeds, what "birds, rocks, and thorns" could hinder the children's full development?

15. In this chapter the author says that God's work cannot be done without waste taking place.
    a. What is your opinion?
    b. What do the following passages say about it?
       Matt. 2. 16;   Matt. 27. 3-5.

SPECIAL NOTE A.

The Interpretation of the Parables by the Early Church

I CAN WE FIND OUT JESUS' OWN INTERPRETATION OF HIS PARABLES?

We have seen (p. 28) that many people think that the interpretation of the parable of a Farmer and his Harvest which is given in Mark 4. 13–20 may be an interpretation given by the early Christians. They think that these verses probably do not give us Jesus' own interpretation. It is natural, therefore, that we should ask the question at the head of this paragraph. We ask this question about all the parables and not about one only. But it is a difficult question to answer.

One difficulty is that the parables were not written down in the same way in all the Gospels. An example is the parable about Men going to the Magistrate. In Luke 12. 54-59 it is an urgent warning: "Why do you not know how to interpret the present time?" But in Matt. 5. 23-26 it is more like a message of encouragement, "Be reconciled to your brother." Readers ask, "Which of these was the teaching that Jesus Himself intended to give?"

In order to answer questions like this one, we have to consider how the parables were written down.

II HOW WERE THE PARABLES WRITTEN DOWN?

Jesus told His parables in conversation with many sorts of people. He did not write them down Himself, and, as far as we know, no one else wrote them down at that time. Immediately after His Resurrection and Ascension, it is likely that His followers still wrote nothing down (probably because they expected that He would return very soon). But they told the parables to other people, and these people used the parables when they preached in public.

But there came a time when Christian preachers needed a handbook about the actions and sayings of Jesus. So St Mark and others wrote something down. This writing was probably done between the year 65 A.D. (i.e. about 35 years after Jesus' Resurrection) and about the year 90 A.D. As it was a long time since Jesus had spoken the parables, these writers probably had to depend chiefly on what people remembered and on what preachers were saying about them. There may also have been a small amount of written material which they could use.

This way was successful because the parables are stories or proverbs. People were able to remember them well and to pass them on to other people. It is far easier to remember stories or proverbs than other sayings. So when we read the parables in the Gospels we know we are reading stories which Jesus told.

But there were difficulties. It was hard to know exactly what words Jesus had used and to whom He had spoken each parable. As we have seen, everyone did not agree about this.

There was also another difficulty. Preachers did not only tell the stories of the parables: they had also begun to interpret them to meet the needs of their own people. This was of course a good thing to do: it is the preacher's work to do this today. But those who heard them could not know if the interpretation which the preacher gave was the interpretation that Jesus Himself had given, or was the preacher's own.

This was also a difficulty for the writers of the Gospels. As we have seen, they also obtained much of their information from Christian preaching. We ask, "Were they themselves able to tell if an interpretation was Jesus' own or the preacher's?" We also ask, "When we read a parable with its interpretation in one of the Gospels, are we reading the interpretation of Jesus, or a later interpretation?"

III JESUS' OWN INTERPRETATIONS, OR LATER INTERPRETATIONS?

Books have been written recently in which it is said that some of the interpretations which are given in the Gospels are later interpretations. Why do they say this?

1. Some parables which Jesus told to the Pharisees seem to have been written down in the Gospels as if they had been told to the disciples. E.g. according to St Luke the Parable of the Lost Sheep was told to the Pharisees as a severe warning to them (Luke 15. 1, 2); but St Matthew says it was told to the disciples to teach them about God's love (Matt. 18. 1, 12-14). It looks as if St Matthew's interpretation is a later one. (We are reminded that those who wrote down the Gospels obtained their information from preachers, and it was natural that preachers should interpret parables as messages for Christians rather than for Pharisees.)

It seems, then, that some parables which have been written down as if they were told to the disciples were really told by Jesus to His enemies. If this is so, we must remember it as we ask the question, "What was Jesus' own interpretation?"

2. Details seem to have been added to what Jesus said. One example of this is the parable of a Host and his Guests. Matt. 22. 1-14 has a long story in which some of the guests killed the servants who were sent to invite them. Then the host set fire to the town where the guests lived. Later, some other guests were sent away because they were

wearing unsuitable clothes. Luke 14. 16-24 has a much simpler story, and probably gives the parable as Jesus told it.

If this is so, then in studying parables, we shall find Jesus' own story by choosing the simpler one.

3. Some of the parables in which Jesus was giving a warning seem to have been interpreted later as parables of encouragement. We have already noticed the parable of Men going to the Magistrate. In Luke 12. 54-59 it seems to be chiefly a parable of urgent warning in which Jesus was teaching, "Receive God's forgiveness before it is too late." But in Matt. 5. 25 the chief message is, "Live at peace with other people." A change seems to have taken place. Perhaps preachers found that urgent warnings were less suitable for their people, because the Second Coming had not occurred and seemed far off. Encouragement to be faithful was a more suitable lesson.

If this change took place, then we shall find Jesus' own interpretation of some parables by remembering that Jesus did frequently preach, "Change your ways before it is too late."

4. Some parables seem to have been interpreted as allegories by the later preachers. This is discussed in Special Note B.

If this is so, then we shall usually find out Jesus' own interpretation by reading the story as a parable rather than as an allegory. (But we do not say that Jesus *never* used allegories.)

5. Later preachers seem sometimes to have placed an interpretation, or several interpretations, at the end of a parable. These interpretations show how Christian leaders, with God's guidance, applied the parables to meet the needs of their people. God was in Christ: He is also in Christ's preachers.

An example of this is the parable of a Clever Agent (Luke 16.1-13). The story is in vv. 1-8a, but then follow three different interpretations in vv. 8b-13.

These extra verses may, of course, have been the words of Jesus Himself. But if so, He probably spoke them at other times. It is unlikely that He gave three different interpretations of a story when He told it.

Whether these extra verses were later interpretations or were the words of Jesus Himself, we are likely to find the central message by studying the parable itself rather than the additional verses.

IV WHAT ARE WE TO SAY
TO THESE SUGGESTIONS?

First we should see these suggestions as attempts to find out the teaching of Jesus Himself, i.e. the teaching He had in mind when He first told the parables. Nothing is more important than this. This is the reason why the question has been repeated in this Note: "Is it possible that later preachers put their own interpretations on this parable in one of these ways?"

Secondly, we cannot prove that later preachers did so. We can say it is "likely" or "unlikely". For instance, in cases where the Gospels give two interpretations of one parable, this does not prove that one is Jesus' own and that the other is not. It is possible that Jesus Himself used the parable in different ways, according to the people He was speaking to. So what has been written above is to be regarded only as a number of suggestions. But they have to be considered seriously.

STUDY SUGGESTIONS FOR SPECIAL NOTE A

Word Study

1. Which *three* of the following words or phrases help to explain the meaning of the word "interpretation" as it is used in this Note?
   application   sermon   contradiction   interference
   explanation   translation from one language to another

2. The words "warning" and "encouragement" are used in this chapter. Give examples from everyday life to show the difference in meaning between them.

Review of Content

3. In what way is the account of the parable of Men going to the Magistrate in Luke 12. 54-59 different from the account of the same parable in Matthew 5. 23-26?

4. *a.* Why did Jesus' followers not write down the parables as soon as He had told them?
   b. Why did Christians afterwards write down the parables?

5. "When we read the parables in the Gospels we know that we are reading stories which Jesus told."
   What makes us think this?

6. To whom did Jesus tell the parable of the Lost Sheep:
   a. According to St Matthew's Gospel?
   b. According to St Luke's Gospel?

7. "Some of the parables in which Jesus was giving a warning seem to have been interpreted later as parables of encouragement" (p. 33). What evidence is there for this statement?

8. Three separate interpretations are given at the end of the parable of a Clever Agent in Luke 16. 1-13.
   Give the verse references for each of these three interpretations.

Bible Study

9. In the following passages it is possible to separate a parable from the verse or verses which have been placed at the end. Say in each case which verses contain the parable itself and which verse or verses have been added to it. ⁾
   a. Luke 12. 16-21;   *b.* Luke 14. 31-33;   *c* Luke 15. 8-10.

10. Say what the word "interpret" means in:
    a. Luke 12. 56 (RSV);   *b.* 1 Cor. 14. 5.

Opinion and Research

11. "If I thought that the interpretation of a parable as it is given in the Gospels was not Jesus' own interpretation I could not trust the Gospels again."
    What would you reply to someone who said this?

12. This Note mentions five ways by which people try to discover the interpretation which Jesus Himself gave to His parables (pp. 32, 33).
    a. Which of these ways do you think is the *most* reliable?
    b. Which do you think is the *least* reliable?
    Give your reasons in each case.

Chapter 4. A Woman and her Money

Luke 15. 8-10
The Parable of the Lost Coin

I OUTLINE

This is another short parable which could be retold in the form of a story:

A woman had ten silver coins and lost one of them. This loss was very serious and she determined not to do anything else until she had found the coin.

First she lit her little olive-oil lamp, because there was no window in her house and no light. Then she made a brush of palm-leaves. But before she started sweeping she shut the door so that she should not sweep the coin out of the house by mistake. Then she began sweeping the trodden-down earth floor.

But the lamp gave very little light, and for a long time she had no success. Then suddenly she heard the noise of the coin being knocked against the wall, and she knew that the brush had touched it. She bent down and picked it up out of the dust. She was so happy that she ran out of the house and told her nearest neighbours that she had found it. They came back to her house with her, and laughed and talked about it together.

II SEEING THE ORIGINAL SITUATION

The situation

St Luke says that this parable was told to the scribes and Pharisees. (The parable of the Lost Sheep was told at the same time.) They had complained that Jesus was encouraging "sinners" to be in His company. This parable was His answer.

The Jews used the word "sinners" in different ways at that time. They used it for people whose lives were evil. See Luke 18. 11. But they also used it for those who could not keep all the Jewish religious laws because of their work. The tax-collectors were an example of such people. They were Jews who were paid by the Romans to collect taxes from the Jews. In doing this work they broke the Jewish law because they had to meet Romans, and Romans (being "Gentiles") were regarded as "unclean". (There was another reason why tax-collectors were called "sinners": because they were helping a foreign government to collect its money and this was thought unpatriotic.)

So "sinners" means all the people who were despised, and treated as inferior and "outcasts".

It was these people with whom Jesus was associating. His enemies were especially angry because He kept on meeting such people even when they did not change their way of living or their place of work. He seemed to enjoy being with them. They said, "A person who is continually in the company of such people cannot be God's messenger."

Jesus therefore told this parable in order to say this:

"It is God's way to go and look for people who are despised or whose lives have gone wrong. But you do not understand His ways. This is the reason why you do not understand what I do and why you attack me. It is you who must change your ways. Stop despising these people. Treat them as sons of God and as your fellow-men."

Suggested Application

The chief message of the parable is about God, although there are also lessons about those whose lives are bad and lessons about people who regard themselves as superior.

1. God treats us all as people who *belong to Him*.

The woman went on looking for the coin because it belonged to her. We belong to God, and this is the reason why He notices our troubles and our successes and is concerned about them.

2. *God looks for us*, and goes on looking for us when we are "lost". (We are using the word "lost" here to mean sinful.) Before Jesus came the Jews had known very well that God was ready to welcome back sinners who repented. ("Seek the Lord while he may be found, call upon him while he is near." Isaiah 55. 6.) But what they understood less clearly was that God is the one who takes action in order to bring us back to fellowship with Him. This is the teaching of this parable.

Jesus also taught this by doing it. First He lived among men for twenty years while He was working as a carpenter. So He knew what we are like: He knew what problems and failures we have. Then, when He began His ministry, He still lived among people who were sinful. He did not wait for them to come to Him. For example, He saw Zacchaeus in the tree and said, "Zacchaeus, I must stay at your house today." (Luke 19. 5.)

3. It is *important to God* when we are "found" after we have been "lost". At the end of this parable Jesus said, "There is joy before the angels of God over one sinner who repents." This is also shown by the parables of the Lost Sheep and of the Prodigal Son. (*Note* that when we say that it is "important to God" we do not mean that God becomes greater. Nor does He become less if we remain lost. Nothing can make God greater or less.)

The Gospels show that it was also important to Jesus Christ when someone was "found". When Zacchaeus was visited by Jesus and decided to change his way of living, Jesus said, "Today salvation has

C

come to this house . . . the Son of Man came to seek and to save the lost.'' (See Luke 19. 1-10.)

4. The followers of Jesus are to *share this attitude* which He had towards "sinners". As we have seen, this is what Jesus was chiefly saying to the Pharisees. How can Christians despise the very same people whose company Jesus enjoyed! This teaching is especially seen in the Parable of an Employer and his Workmen. See chapter 5.

III SEEING OUR OWN SITUATION

There are several human situations which could be considered as we read this parable. The one which is chosen here is the situation of being "lost".

Who are the "lost"?

We saw that the word "sinners" was used to mean different things. In the same way there are many different kinds of people who are "lost" in God's eyes. For example:

Those who have had little or no opportunity of loving and obeying God.

Those who have had a good opportunity of loving and obeying, but have refused to.

Those who belong to the Church but without love, not seeing how much they need God, or not being willing to see this.

From this it is plain that the "lost" in this parable are ourselves, whoever we are.

To sum up:

1. All humans are "lost".

2. We all have to put ourselves in the position where we can be "found" or "saved". At a football match where there were crowds of spectators, a very small boy became separated from his father as they were leaving the ground. He told a man and was taken to the ticket office. When someone asked him if he was "lost", he said, "Yes; but this is where my father will find me."

3. It needs choice and decision to put ourselves in the position where we can be "found". The first time we make the choice it is sometimes said that we have been "converted".

4. But the choice has to be renewed again and again afterwards. Some Christians are described in Acts 2. 47 as "those who were being saved", i.e. who "kept on being found".

Here are some examples of people who have this choice to make:

The first is a Church worker who works hard but without joy. He is not an easy person to work with, but no one tells him this because it does not seem that he would accept it. He is inside the Church, just as the coin was lost inside the woman's house. He is lost because he

"All humans are 'lost'. . . . We all have to put ourselves in the position where we can be found."

This police officer from a Pacific Island force was glad to be able to help the lost boy go to the place where his father could find him.

is in one way separated from His God. Yet he does not know that he is separated. He need not remain separated.

The second is a regular member of the Church, too. She is a happy and popular member. She was brought up by Christian parents. But she has no faith of her own: she has borrowed the beliefs of her parents and does not know that they are not her own.

The third is a member of the Church who was responsible for a large sum of money. Now he cannot account for a huge amount. An enquiry is held and he is dismissed from his post. He is overcome by shame and by guilt, and says that he cannot be forgiven. A friend explains that Jesus came to rescue people who felt just as he felt, "lost" and unworthy. Will he take this offer from God of a new start?

The fourth is a boy who is always in trouble with the police. He has no father and no mother. He has no connection with the Church. He gets work occasionally in the city where he lives. He is like the coin in this parable in this way: it is not really his fault that he is "lost". He thinks that Church people look down on him. He does not know that God does not look down on him. When a Christian meets him and shows him friendship, will he be able to see that God also offers him friendship?

The fifth is a Christian teacher who is serious about his religion. But he finds as he grows older that he is always falling into the same bad habits. He is beginning to say, "Well, this is how I have been made." Will he go on accepting God's help and forgiveness each time he fails? Or will he despair?

NOTES

a. Other parables of this kind. Of the parables studied in this book, this is the first in which Jesus teaches about God's care for "sinners" and calls on religious people to treat "sinners" in the way that He treats them. See also chapters 5, 6, and 7, and Note **a.** on p. 46.

b. Ten silver coins (v. 8). This was the money which she had in the house.

Some people think that these coins were the coins which were a woman's dowry. It was the custom for a woman to wear these on her head-dress, and one could have come unsewn. If this were so, the coin she had lost would be even more precious to her than an ordinary coin.

c. There is joy before the angels of God (v. 10). This simply means that "God is joyful." It was the custom among the Jews to show reverence for the Name of God by saying "the angels of God" or "the throne of God" instead of using the name "God".

STUDY SUGGESTIONS FOR CHAPTER 4

Word Study

1. Before Jesus told this parable the Jews used the word "sinner" to describe different sorts of people. Which *three* out of the following words and phrases show what these different sorts were?
   prostitutes   religious people who are not loving   thieves
   everybody   Jews who mix with Gentiles

2. The words "be converted" are used in this chapter. The same words are used to translate the Greek word *straphete* in Matt. 18. 3 (AV).
   a. Compare this with the translation of it given in:
      i another English version;
      ii any other language you know.
   b. In one East African language the word used for "conversion" means "entering the territory of another chief and so putting myself under his authority". Is this a good translation? Give reasons for your answer.

Review of Content

3. Why did the woman in the parable have to light a lamp before she could find the coin?

4. What sort of coin did the woman lose?

5. To whom did Jesus tell the parable of the Lost Coin?

6. Why did the Jews regard tax-collectors as "sinners"?

7. "Before Jesus came the Jews had known that God was ready to welcome back sinners who repented."
   What new or additional teaching did Jesus give about God's attitude to "sinners"?

8. We read in the chapter of a Church worker who was "lost". What were the outward signs of this?

9. Why did Luke write "before the angels of God" instead of simply writing "before God" in Luke 15. 10?

Bible Study

10. "God treats us as people who belong to Him."
    If you were preaching on this subject, which *two* of the following texts would you regard as the most suitable? Give reasons for your answer.
       Exodus 24. 8;   Romans 8. 39;   John 15. 15.

11. What change in his way of living did Zacchaeus make when he had been "found" or "saved" (Luke 19. 1-10)?

12. "God looks for us."
 Which of the following passages expresses this truth most clearly?
 Give reasons for your answer.
 Ezekiel 34. 11-16; Job 37. 21-24.

Opinion and Research

13. Remembering the story of the boy lost at the football match:
 a. Who can help "lost" people?
 b. In what way can they help them?

14. We read in the chapter of a girl whose religion was borrowed from
 her parents.
 a. What are the results of having such a religion?
 b. How could the girl be helped to have a religion of her own?

15. We read in the chapter of a boy who was in trouble, and the
 author says that it was "not really his fault".
 a. Is it ever true to say that "So-and-so went wrong but it was not
 his fault"?
 b. If it was not the boy's fault, whose fault do you think it may
 have been?

16. What practical steps can a Christian take who finds that he is
 "always falling into the same bad habits" (p. 40)?

17. In the Outline on p. 36 the author has enlarged the parable
 contained in Luke 15. 8 and 9. What are the advantages and
 disadvantages of "enlarging" a parable in this way? In your
 answers give examples from the Outline.

Chapter 5. An Employer and his Workmen

Matt. 20. 1-16
The Parable of the Labourers in the Vineyard

I OUTLINE

There was once a man who owned a vineyard and needed labourers. Very early one morning he engaged some men and agreed to pay them the usual wage for a day's work. But he needed many more, and so three times over he came back to the market-place, and engaged more men each time. He made an agreement with them about wages.

At 5 p.m. there was an urgent need for more workmen. Probably it was harvest time and therefore important to harvest the grapes and press them before the heavy rains began. So another group of men was engaged.

An hour later the owner told his manager to give the men their wages. To the surprise of everyone, all the men were given the same amount: they were all given a full day's pay. Those who had done a full day's work regarded this as very unfair. They marched to the owner and complained. The owner said to one of them, "My friend, I am not cheating you. I have given you what I promised to give you. Don't be jealous of those who only worked for an hour. You must allow me to have pity on their poverty if I want to."

II SEEING THE ORIGINAL SITUATION

The situation
Who listened to this parable the first time that Jesus told it? Why did He tell it? St Matthew has not told us. In his Gospel he has placed this parable after a conversation between Jesus and His disciples. But this does not mean that the two took place on the same day.

But the story itself helps us to answer those questions. We notice that in vv. 10-12 those who had worked all day were angry with the owner. They were angry because he had been very generous to those who had only done one hour's work. This is the part of the story which surprises us and makes us think. We ask, "Why did the owner do that?"

So it is here that we are given the reason why Jesus told the parable. There were Jews who were like the angry men of the parable, e.g. the Pharisees. They thought that because of their good deeds God ought to give them special rewards. So they criticized Jesus when He welcomed the despised people and showed them generosity and kindness.

In this parable, then, Jesus was chiefly saying this:
"God is merciful, and I am merciful. He values those whom you call

outcasts or 'sinners'. You think this outlook of mercy is wrong. But it is your outlook that is wrong and needs to be changed."

Suggested Application

1. God's generosity.

In the parable the employer was sorry for the men who were poor, and treated them generously. So God is both sorry for all who are in trouble or in sin, and treats them with generosity.

Let us ask how God treats "bad" people. He treats them better than they deserve. He gives them His love and His forgiveness. This is what they need, but they have not earned it. It is His free gift. It is what is often called God's "grace".

"Bad people" does not mean only people whose sins are known to everybody: it means also ourselves whenever we fail to be the kind of people God has intended us to be. It is *we* who read this who are being treated better than we deserve.

But His "grace" has to be accepted. The men who were in the market-place at 5 p.m. had to choose if they would go with the employer or stay where they were.

2. God's agreement with men.

The employer in the parable said to those men who complained, "Did you not agree with me about your wages?" (v. 13). And it was so: they had agreed to work for exactly the amount which he gave them. So a Christian's life is founded on an agreement between himself and God. This agreement is sometimes called a "covenant" in which God has made His promises to look after His people, and the Christian has made his promises to serve God.

When we are tempted to complain that another group of people has been better treated than we have, when we feel that God has not been fair to us, we remember these words, "Did you not agree with me?" God never promised that Christians would be either rich or successful or without suffering.

3. A warning against the outlook of the Pharisees.

This is the chief message of the parable and we shall study it further in part III of this chapter.

We have already seen that the Pharisees and others thought that they themselves were "holy" and that certain other people were "sinners". In their minds there was a clear division between the two: they themselves were "in" God's Kingdom, the others were "outside" it; they were "first", the others were "last". They themselves were "superior", the others were "inferior".

We must remember that many of the Pharisees were good people. And yet they made serious mistakes:

a. They forgot that in God's eyes the people whom they called "sinners" were often more humble and more ready to listen to God than they were themselves.

b. They despised "sinners" and kept apart from them.

Jesus behaved quite differently. He met the despised people and enjoyed being with them. He did not condemn them, but did what He could to give them a new start in their lives. He tells us to behave like this also.

III SEEING OUR OWN SITUATION

In the parable, those who worked all day felt superior to those who only worked for one hour. They wanted these others to be treated differently. They were angry when they saw that these others were receiving the same pay as they received themselves.

1. This is a situation in which we often find ourselves. We all belong to some group which is separated from the people of another group: we are tempted to feel superior to those of the other group. Here are some examples:

In Japan the *'eta'* or *'buraku'* people (the leather workers) are treated as outcasts.

In most European countries there are boys and girls between the ages of 14 and 20 who dress and behave in a way that offends older people. There is division between them and the older people. Each group seems to despise the other.

There are many countries in which the people of one race or tribe treat the people of another race or tribe as inferior.

In many places those who have been to prison are often despised and regarded as "outcast" by others.

In a few places those who are Christians treat non-Christians as less important than themselves: in other places it is the Christians who are treated as the "second-class citizens".

Often those who have received modern education treat those who have not been to school as inferior.

Whenever we are in a situation like this, we are given a choice between two ways of behaving. This choice comes to us in different ways. For example:

a. Am I going to keep myself separate from the people of this "other" group *or* am I going to associate with them?

I am a senior member of my village. Do I speak only with people of my own age, *or* do I take the trouble to find out what younger people are thinking and saying and wanting?

I am a member of the Church. Are all my friends Church members *or* do I make friends with those who do not belong to the Church?

45

b. Do we who are Christians plan our Church services only for Church members *or* do we prepare also for those who are outside the Church? Do newcomers receive a warm welcome when they come to Church? Do people who are not well dressed receive as good a welcome as the richer people? Can newcomers understand what is taking place in a service?

c. Do I judge these "other" people, *or* do I help to change their circumstances?

I shall be tempted to judge them. But I can, on the other hand, fight against the things that make their lives poor or bad, e.g. unjust laws, disease, ignorance, lack of work, the wrong kind of education, lack of houses. Of course people can live good lives in spite of such things. But it is more difficult for people living in bad conditions to live the lives that God meant them to live.

2. The way in which we behave towards these "other people" is important for our own lives. If we make the right choices in these situations, we are sharing in the way which Jesus took. If we make the wrong choices, it is our own lives which we are spoiling. The parable is, indeed, a warning.

NOTES

a. Another parable. The parable about Two Debtors (Luke 7. 41, 42) seems to have been told for the same reason. Simon was a Pharisee who criticized Jesus because He received the gifts of a despised woman. So Jesus told him about two men who both owed money. Both of them were let off their debts by the generous man to whom the money was owed. The one who had owed him the most was the most grateful. Jesus said, "This woman has been forgiven more than you have. So she is more grateful to God than you are. She is thus the more acceptable to God. It is not for you to criticize me or her."

b. Parables of Surprise. In Matt. 20. 1–16 we expect those who have been working for a long time to receive more than those who only worked a little. But we are surprised to see that they do not. There are several other parables which contain surprises like this. In each one, there are two people (or two groups of people). Those who expected to receive special attention do not receive it: the others do receive it.

In the parable of a Host and his Guests (Luke 14. 15-24) those who were expected to come and enjoy the supper-party do not come: those who were not invited at first are the ones who come. This is what actually happened when Jesus began His work. Most of the religious people refused to accept what He said: it was the despised "sinners" who welcomed Him and were "acceptable" to God.

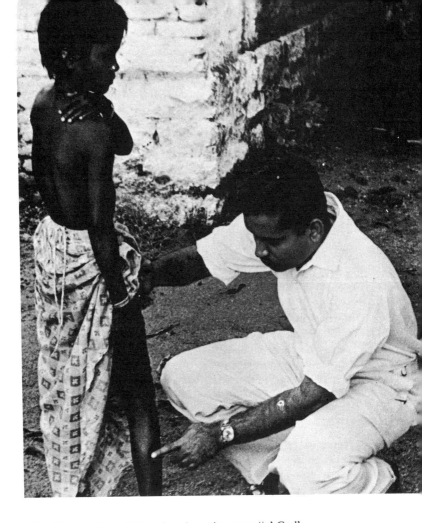

"The Pharisees thought that they themselves were 'in' God's Kingdom, while others were 'outside'. But Jesus behaved quite differently. He met the despised people . . . and did what He could to give them a new start in life."

This little girl is 12 years old. She has leprosy, and the people of her village have chased her out and will not give her food or shelter. But the doctor knows she can be cured, and he treats her just as carefully as he treats any other patient.

In the parable of a Father and his Sons (Luke 15. 11-32), we expect the younger son to be blamed and the older son to be praised. This does not happen. The younger is the one who takes part in the meal, the older son is absent.

In the parable of the Lost Sheep (Luke 15. 3-7), we expect the shepherd to stay with the ninety-nine sheep to look after them, but he leaves them and goes in search of one single lost one.

Jesus explains all this in Matt. 21. 31, 32: "Tax-gatherers and prostitutes are entering the Kingdom of God ahead of you. For when John came to show you the right way to live, you did not believe him, but the tax-gatherers and prostitutes did" (NEB).

c. The kingdom of heaven is like . . . . (v. 1). We have already seen that the words "Kingdom of Heaven" mean "God's authority or kingship over people". They describe what God does, not a place.

In v. 1 this ruling of God seems to be compared to the employer himself. But this is not so. When we have read the whole parable we see that the words mean, "God rules over mankind in the same way in which this employer distributed his wages on that day", that is to say, with authority and with mercy.

We shall see in chapter 6 that in Matt. 22. 1, 2 we are not being taught that the Kingdom of Heaven is like a king. The words mean, "The way that God rules over men is like the way in which this king treated his guests that day."

d. Denarius (v. 2). This is sometimes translated "penny". It was a Roman coin given to an unskilled labourer for one day's work. It is hard to translate this word today in any country where wages are rising all the time.

e. Each of them received a denarius (v. 9). As we have seen, these words show us something about the way in which God shows His generosity to men.

They are certainly *not* words of advice given by Jesus to employers. He was not telling them how to pay their labourers. If an employer today gave a whole day's pay to workmen who only began work at 5 p.m. he might not see anyone at work the next morning! He would also have trouble with the Agricultural Workers' Union. Jesus did not come to give advice of that kind.

If we want to understand this employer, we must notice that he was an employer who behaved more like a father than an employer. Jesus did not mean that all employers ought to do exactly as the employer in the parable did.

This reminds us that we may interpret a parable quite wrongly unless
a. we read the whole story, rather than one sentence only;

b. we note the special reason why Jesus told this story;

c. we study the teaching of the rest of the New Testament along with it.

f. So the last shall be first and the first last (v. 16). Although this saying comes at the end of the parable, it does not seem to fit the parable. The "last" did not become the "first" in the story. Everyone received the same. No one was first.

In the Authorized Version there is a second part to this verse: "Many be called, but few chosen." But this does not fit the parable either. There was no choosing of a "few" out of "many" who were called. All who were called were given work and wages.

It seems that Jesus spoke both these sayings at a different time, and that when He told the parable they did not belong to it. The first saying is found in Mark 10. 31. The second is in Matt. 22. 14. See p.33, numbered paragraph 5.

STUDY SUGGESTIONS FOR CHAPTER 5

Word Study

1. Write two sentences each showing the meaning of the word "outcast".

2. *a.* Describe briefly the actions of an employer who is "generous" to his workmen.
   b. Describe the actions of one who is "fair".

3. "Superior" and "inferior" are a pair of "opposites". Give three other pairs of opposites which have the same or nearly the same meaning.

Review of Content

4. What did Jesus want His hearers to learn through the parable of an Employer and his Workmen?

5. In what way did Jesus behave differently from some of the Pharisees?

6. What is meant by the phrase "parables of surprise"?

7. The parable of an Employer and his Workmen is about God's "covenant" with men.
   a. What is God's part in the covenant, according to the teaching of this parable?
   b. What is man's part?

8. Which people in this parable show that "grace" or "generosity" has to be accepted?

Bible Study

9. Read Luke 18. 10-14 and Matt. 21. 28-31. These are two more "parables of surprise". Say in each case:
   a. what the hearers would *expect* to happen,
   b. what actually *does* happen,
   c. what we can learn from these "surprises".

Opinion and Research

10. This chapter gives several examples in which people of one group regard those of another group as "inferior". Give three other examples that can be found in your own country.

11. What organizations exist in your own country, or in another, to help people who are in "inferior" situations? Say where you obtained your information.

12. What do you understand by the words, "The last shall be first and the first last"?

13. What questions should we ask ourselves when we find ourselves thinking that we are being unfairly treated by God or by other people?

14. What special message may Gentiles living in the first century A.D. have found in the parable of an Employer and his Workmen?

15. "Educated people are superior to uneducated ones."
    a. Do you agree? Give reasons for your answer.
    b. What can school education *not* give?

16. An English proverb says, "It's never too late to mend."
    a. In what way is the teaching of the parable of an Employer and his Workmen like the teaching of this proverb?
    b. Do you know a similar proverb in another language? If so, translate it into English, and write a short parable of your own to illustrate the truth that it teaches.

Chapter 6.   A Father and his Sons

Luke 15. 11-32
The Parable of the Prodigal Son

I OUTLINE

A man had two sons. One day the younger of the two demanded the share of his father's property which would belong to him when his father died. His father gave it to him, and after a few days the boy left home on a long journey.

Here he wasted the money and lived a wild life. When the money was all spent, there was a famine, and he began to be in serious need. He found some work in looking after the pigs of a farmer in that district. But there was nothing which he could eat.

At last he was so hungry and so hopeless that he started to consider who he was and what sort of person he had become. He saw that he was poorer than the poorest of his father's servants. Then he decided to return home. He planned to admit that he had done wrong and to ask his father to employ him as a servant, since he could not expect to be treated as a son any longer.

So he made the long journey home. But before he could reach the house, his father saw him. He saw the boy's misery, and ran down the road and welcomed him with affection. The boy began to speak of the wrong that he had done, but before he could ask to be employed as a servant, his father called for a robe of honour and put it on him. Then he gave him a ring and sandals to show that he was fully accepted as his son. And a feast was prepared so that everyone could share in his father's joy.

The other son had been working on the farm. As he returned to the house he heard the singing and the hand-clapping, and asked what had happened. His father came out and begged him to join in the feast. But he said, "I have worked for you for years, yet you never made a feast for me. Now you welcome this son of yours who has wasted your money." Then his father said gently, "My boy, of course we must welcome him home. He is not only 'my son' as you call him; he is your brother. Come inside and share my joy. The one that was lost has now been found."

II SEEING THE ORIGINAL SITUATION

The situation
St Luke put this story alongside the stories of the Lost Sheep and Lost Coin, and it is likely that Jesus told all three for the same reasons.

We saw that He told those parables as a reply to the scribes and Pharisees. They had become troubled because Jesus was associating with "sinners". His behaviour seemed to them to be wicked, and they criticized Him severely for it. By means of these parables He explained why He welcomed such people. He called on the scribes and Pharisees also to share in God's love and His care for "sinners" and despised people.

So the first time that Jesus told this parable, He told it (as He told those other parables) to His enemies. It seems that He was asking them to compare:

a. the attitude of the father towards the boy, and

b. the attitude of the elder brother who refused to give the boy a welcome. Jesus was saying:

"Will you have the outlook of the elder brother or the attitude of the father towards 'sinners'? Are you going to stand apart from people, or will you share in God's love towards them? If you share in God's love, you will also share in His joy when they return to fellowship with Him."

We must notice that the parable was not only a rebuke to His enemies. It was also an appeal, spoken in love. Jesus longed that they should change their ways. This is shown by the gentle way in which the father spoke to the elder brother, "My boy . . . ." (v. 31).

Suggested Application

The message of this parable is not very different from the message of the parables of the Lost Sheep and the Lost Coin. We shall notice here especially:

1. God and His love.
2. People without Love.
3. People without God.

1. God and His love. The father in the story showed his love for the boy in many ways: by giving him freedom to leave home although he knew the boy might misuse that freedom, by running to welcome the boy back in spite of his behaviour, by his joy when the boy returned. In noticing this and also the teaching given by Jesus at other times we learn what God's love for mankind is like.

a. He loves us all the time. He loves us even while we are doing wrong. He hates our sinfulness but never stops loving us ourselves. We do not cease to be His sons even when we are bad sons.

b. He offers to rescue us and He offers forgiveness all the time. (But we cannot receive it until we are sorry for wrong-doing and sincerely intend to change our ways.)

c. He does not wait for us to earn His love or forgiveness. He offers them freely. We see this clearly when we compare this parable with a Buddhist story about a lost son. In the Buddhist story the father hides from the son when he returns, and orders his servants to test the boy in different ways to see if he has fully repented of wasting his money. When the boy has passed these tests, the father receives him back. This story shows the way that people usually expect God to behave. So people try to earn God's love by being good or by making sacrifices. But God's love cannot be earned: it can only be received thankfully and humbly.

d. If we read nothing but this story we might think that it is easy for God to forgive. But if we read the story along with the rest of the New Testament we know that this is not so. In the rest of the New Testament we are taught that we are forgiven because Jesus died. Jesus Himself said (Mark 10. 45) that He must be offered (as a ransom is offered) before the "many" could be set free from their sin. And when we read of His dying, we are able to see what it cost God to forgive us.

2. People without Love. The attitude of the elder brother reminds us that it is possible to be religious without being loving. So the parable is a warning. We are without love when:

We grow so accustomed to God and His love for us that we are no longer grateful to Him;

We think that God loves us because we are good sons and forget that He loves us simply because we are His sons;

We judge others and fail to care for them in their troubles and in their sins;

We forget that if God is our Father then all His sons are our brothers.

If we are without love in these ways, then we are missing the full life that God meant us to live. We are missing it just as the elder brother cut himself off from the feast. (It is usual to say that the younger son was "lost", and so he was. But the elder brother was "lost" too. He cut himself off from the full life of sharing in the joys and the troubles. of the rest of his family. He failed to "rejoice with those who rejoice" or to "weep with those who weep" (Rom. 12.15).)

3. People without God. From studying the "lost son" in the parable, we learn much about human beings as they try to live without God. (We have already learnt about "lost people" in the parable of the Lost Coin, in chapter 4.) Being "lost" is now considered again in part III of this chapter.

III SEEING OUR OWN SITUATION

1. The boy who was "lost" reminds us of all human sin and suffering. This is a parable, not an allegory, or a sermon, so we shall not expect to be given a full description. But the story does remind us of some ways in which man sins and suffers:

53

"Are you going to stand apart from people, or will you share in God's love for them and 'rejoice with those who rejoice'?"

Kalabit people in Sarawak enjoy welcoming a traveller back to their longhouse.

a. The desire to be free from responsibility.

When the boy demanded his money, he was refusing his duties and responsibilities and discipline at home. So he went away and did what he wanted.

So we human beings want to be free from responsibilities God has given us. People have children but expect the State to teach them good manners. People live in a town but expect other people to make it a good town. People want to be free, but forget that they must give an account to God of how the freedom is used.

b. Self-centredness.

The boy said to his father, "Give me" (v. 12). So people say, "Let the world give me what I want; let other people give me what I think I deserve." Newspapers and advertisements encourage their readers to say this more and more.

c. Disappointment.

The things which the boy received did not last for long. They could not satisfy him. This disappointment comes to anyone who expects that things can themselves bring him peace and joy. An American has recently written, "We Americans have now got everything. Why then are we not satisfied?"

So when we read about this boy, we are not reading about a great sinner, but about ordinary people. Many of us will also find ourselves saying, "I am reading about myself."

2. In the same way, the way in which the boy was rescued may remind us of some ways in which all mankind and we ourselves can be rescued (since it is not an allegory, it will not give us the whole Christian Gospel).

a. He began to know himself. ("He came to himself" v. 17.) He saw what sort of person he was becoming. (Feeding pigs was the work given to those who could not do any other work.) He discovered that his demand of "give me" did not bring the best kind of life.

A man begins to return to fellowship with God when he sees what sort of person he is becoming. One man's prayer was, "O God, I know what I have and what I do. But I don't know what I *am.*"

b. He knew his need. He was hungry and ashamed. So the one thing that is necessary before God can take a man back into fellowship with Himself is that the man should know his need. The person who thinks he can live in his own strength cannot be helped.

c. He remembered his home and wanted to return (v. 18). It is not enough for someone to be in need: that person must know also where his home is. He must be "home-sick" for home. One overseas student in London says that the longing to return home is the thing that helps him to live a good life in London. God Himself is the Father and the Home of every man. ("Dwell in me" John 15. 4, NEB.)

d. He returned to his father in faith. He could not be sure if his father would accept him. ("Treat me as one of your hired servants" v. 19.) But he was welcomed with joy. When someone returns to God, he does so in "faith", i.e. he does so because he relies on God's generosity and forgiveness. He does not return because of what he himself has done.

NOTES

a. Parable, not allegory. This is a parable, and has one chief message which we find by reading the whole story. (We have tried to state this "chief message" in part II of this chapter.)

If it had been an allegory, we should have taken a lesson from each part of the story. We might have said, "The father in the story is God." But we cannot say that. Although the father loved the son, he did not make a journey to find him. But, as we have seen in chapter 4, God does not wait for sinners to return, He goes out to find them.

In the same way we cannot say that when Jesus spoke about the robe and ring and sandals in v. 22, He was thinking of the Bible and Baptism and Holy Communion. Some people have made the story into an allegory and have interpreted these words in this way. But these things are in the story because the story would not be complete without them: they are there to show that the son was given back his old position in the home. See Special Note B, p. 67.

b. The name of this parable. This parable was called the parable of the Prodigal (i.e. wasteful) Son by those who gave us the Authorized Version. It is not the best title for the parable because it draws our attention only to one person in the story. We have seen that Jesus was directing the attention of His hearers to the father and the older brother as well as to the younger son.

c. To feed swine (v. 15). This parable was told to Jews, and among the Jews pigs were considered "unclean" animals. Anyone who fed pigs was breaking the rules of his religion, i.e. he was a "sinner".

d. All that is mine is yours (v. 31) i.e. you have nothing to boast about. You have it because I give it to you and because you are my son.

STUDY SUGGESTIONS FOR CHAPTER 6

Word Study

1. The Greek phrase *eis heauton elthon* in Luke 15. 17 is translated "he came to himself" (RSV). Compare this with the translation given in:
   a. another English version;
   b. any other language you know.

2. We have read in this chapter that God "rescues" His people. Jesus Himself said that He had come to "ransom" us. Give examples from everyday life to show the difference in meaning between the words "rescue" and "ransom".

3. For each of the following words used in this chapter, give another which has the opposite meaning.
   a. responsible   b. self-centred   c. disappointed

4. The boy in the parable "returned to his father in faith" (p. 56). What does "faith" mean in this sentence?

Review of Content

5. a. For what reasons did the younger son decide to go home?
   b. In what ways are the words spoken by him in Luke 15 verse 21 different from his words in verses 18 and 19?

6. Are the following true or untrue? Give reasons for your answer in each case.
   a. God waits for us to earn His forgiveness.
   b. God never stops offering to pardon us.
   c. God continues to care for us even when we are committing sin.
   d. We cannot earn God's love.
   e. It is easy for God to forgive us.

7. What is the difference between the parable of the Father and his Sons and the Buddhist parable given in this chapter?

8. The younger brother was indeed lost. But how far is it true to say that the *elder* brother was also "lost"?

9. Why is it not helpful to say that "the father in this parable stands for God"?

Bible Study

10. Some people have compared this parable to the story of Jonah. Who, in the book of Jonah, can be compared to:
    a. the son who said he had "sinned"?
    b. the elder brother?
    Give chapter and verse from the book of Jonah in each case.

11. Which *two* out of the following passages contain teaching which is like the teaching of the parable of a Father and his Sons?
Psalm 103. 8-14; James 5. 7-11; Psalm 15; Ephesians 2. 4-10.

Opinion and Research

12. *a.* Why does the author say that the Prodigal Son is not a good title for this parable?
b. Suggest two other titles.

13. *a.* Why did the father let the younger son take his share and leave home?
b. Was the father right to do so? Give reasons for your answer.

14. Why do you think Jesus did not end this parable at verse 24?

15. Church people sometimes behave like the elder brother.
a. In what ways?
b. Why do you think they do so?.

16. *a.* Why is it important for us to discover what sort of people we are becoming?
b. How can we discover what we are becoming?

17. Someone who heard this parable said, "It teaches us that it is better to sin and to come back to God than not to sin at all."
a. What is your opinion?
b. What guidance does Romans 6. 1-4 give you?

Chapter 7. A Host and his Guests

Luke 14. 15-24
The Parable of the Great Supper

I OUTLINE

A man was preparing to have a supper party and sent out invitations to a great many people. When the day came and the supper was quite ready, he sent out a second invitation saying, "Everything is ready now." But they did not come. Every one of them sent a message saying that they were engaged in doing other things.

When the messenger told this to the host, the host was angry. He knew that these things did not really prevent them from coming. He could see that they did not want to come.

So he said to the messenger, "We shall have our party in spite of these people. Go and invite in any poor strangers whom you can find." The messenger brought some strangers in, but there was still room. Then the host said, "Go to districts further away from this house and invite still more people. If they are afraid to come to a strange house, persuade them as well as you can." Then he added, "The invited guests have shut themselves out. But we will fill the house with guests of a different kind."

II SEEING THE ORIGINAL SITUATION

The situation

This parable seems to have been told when Jesus went to eat at a Pharisee's house (Luke 14. 1). During the conversation Jesus said to the Pharisee, "When you have a party, invite people who cannot give you any hospitality in return. They are the guests who most need your invitations" (see v. 13). Then one of the guests (who was also a religious man) said, "When God gives His great feast in heaven, we shall accept His invitation gladly!" Then Jesus said to him, "Are you sure that you would accept it? Listen to this story." Then He told them this parable.

This is another parable in which Jesus was teaching His listeners about Himself and His work. He was telling it to people who did not like what He did. Jesus was saying this:

"I mix with people who know that they need God's help, that is, with people whose lives are bad and who break the religious laws. But you think I should not do this. You think that such people should be judged but not rescued. *But these sinners are in a better position to receive what God offers than are many of you religious people.*"

This was very stern teaching to give to the Pharisees when Jesus was being a guest in the house of one of them. Perhaps it made His host very angry. But it was spoken in love, as an appeal to them to change their attitude.

Note that in this chapter we are using St Luke's account of this parable. In St Matthew's Gospel (22. 1-14) the parable is a longer story and is very hard to understand. It seems as if two or three different parables have become mixed together in St Matthew's account.

Suggested application

1. What does God offer to mankind?

This is a story about a feast or a supper party, that is to say, about good food and good fellowship offered to guests by a host. Behind the story is teaching about God and His offer of good things. What are those "good things"?

First, God offers Himself, just as Jesus was offering Himself to those who first heard the parable. We talk of God giving good gifts, but He Himself is the gift. We cannot separate the forgiveness and grace of God from God Himself.

Secondly, when someone accepts Him, that person accepts life of the best kind. He accepts a rich life. It is not a life of continual pleasure but it is always *full*. It is full of joy and pain, of being still and being active; it is full of fellowship with God and full of fellowship with other people; it is full of sorrow for each failure to do God's will, and full of gratitude for each time when He forgives.

Thus God offers us the gift of Himself in the whole of life (and not only through the Sacraments of the Church). This is what the Pharisees did not understand. They thought that God gave Himself only to those who kept His laws. So they thought of God's gift as smaller than it is.

Thirdly, Christians who have received this "fullness" of life (as Jesus called it in John 10. 10, NEB) will make others want it, too. Unfortunately we Christians often let other people think that being a Christian is different from this. After looking at us they think that it is nothing more than (*a*) obeying new rules, or (*b*) not doing what other people do, or (*c*) feeling guilty more often than others do, or (*d*) going to Church. if so, then it is not surprising when they do not want to be Christians!

2. Who can accept what God offers?

The parable shows that no one accepts the gift that God offers who is satisfied with his own life. But anyone who knows that he is in need is able to accept it. The supper party was enjoyed by poor people and lame and blind people. They were different from each other in all ways except one way: they were all in need. They were all dependent on the host: they were hungry and thirsty for the supper he offered.

Jesus gave the same teaching in the Beatitudes when He said, "How blest are those who know that they are poor . . . . How blest are those who hunger and thirst" (Matt. 5. 3, 6, NEB).

This hunger is the thing that God looks for in people who want His gifts. We have seen this already as we read about the "lost son" (Chapter 6). We think that we can bribe Him or pay Him with our good deeds or hard work. But His gifts are real gifts, and are for everyone who is hungry. This is what a girl in a boarding-school seems to have discovered. In a letter to an old teacher, she told how she was always getting into trouble although she tried to please her teachers and God. "Then," she said, "I came to the end of myself." We do not know what happened between her and God; but she was hungry, she found that she could not get on without Him. And the staff of the school noticed a difference in her behaviour after that time; her work was more carefully done and she was quicker to notice when other girls needed to be helped.

3. Those who do not accept God's gifts.

In the parable the host did not send away those who were invited at first: they kept themselves away. This is what happens when we continue to refuse what God offers. He does not condemn us to suffering. We condemn ourselves. We shut ourselves out. We do not only refuse opportunities of worshipping Him. We also refuse His forgiveness and the peace and strength which He offers to us as we go about our day's work.

III SEEING OUR OWN SITUATION

Those who were first invited to the supper party were in a situation which we know very well: they had to choose between doing something that was good and doing the best thing.

Each of these people chose to do something that was good. Two of them had developed their farms. One had done it by buying more land, the other by buying more bullocks for ploughing. These two wanted the pleasure of looking at what they had bought. The other just wanted to be with the wife he had married the day before. These are all good things to do.

But their host offered them something which *at that time* was even better. At that time it was even better to go to the party to which they had been invited a long time before. They were quite free to choose and they chose not to have the best.

We know this kind of situation. We often have to make this kind of choice. And it is a choice given to us by God Himself. It is not hard to think of examples of this:

"We often refuse the best things because they are unknown to us . . . We show 'faith' when we choose the best kind of life because Jesus has told us that it is the best. But we cannot know that it is the best till we have tried it."

For many generations the people of this South Indian village have suffered from tuberculosis and other infectious diseases, but often they try to hide their illness. When the health officer visits them they are afraid to accept treatment, and refuse his advice about how to conquer the disease and become strong and healthy.

62

It is good for a man to work hard at his job and to earn money. But there are times when it is even better for him to stop working for a time and to earn less money, in order to be with his wife and family.

It is good to be an active minister and to take pains in the preparation of sermons. But sometimes such a person is shown that something even better than this is possible for him: e.g. he could learn to be a gentle and forgiving person. (This kind of choice is not given once only. God offers it to us many times.)

It is good for a Church congregation to pay its contributions regularly and to repair and decorate its church. But sometimes a congregation believes that other things are even more important to it; e.g. that it should become a fellowship of men and women who really trust each other, and who offer real friendship to newcomers.

NOTE: When we choose between good things and things which are even better, we are often choosing between good things which we know and the best things which we do not know. We often refuse the best things because they are unknown to us. It is like a man who always writes with the same kind of pen, and finds it satisfactory. Someone shows him a new kind and says, "Try this. I think you will find it even better." But he smiles and says, "No, I think I will just use the one that I know."

We show "faith" when we choose the best kind of life because Jesus has told us that it is the best. But we cannot know it is the best until we have tried it. How do we try it? By behaving as if Jesus' words were true and watching the results. Here is one example. A man works in an office with other people whom he does not like very much. For one whole day he treats them as people who are loved by God, because Jesus has said that this is what they are. He finds that as a result he is blaming them less when things go wrong. He is more ready to accept his own share of blame. He finds that this is indeed a better way of living.

NOTES

a. Other Parables. There are other parables which are like this one in certain ways. In them Jesus seems to have been teaching about God's love for people although they were "sinners". He was warning religious people not to despise them:

A Woman and her Money (Luke 15. 8-10. See Chapter 4).
A Shepherd and his Sheep (Luke 15. 3-7.)
An Employer and his Workmen (Matt. 20. 1-16. See Chapter 5).
Two Debtors (Luke 7. 41, 42.)
A Father and his Sons (Luke 15. 11-32. See Chapter 6).
Two Sons (Matt. 21. 28-31).
The Pharisee and the Tax-Collector (Luke 18. 9-14).

In three other parables Jesus seems to have been saying this: "Even a man in bed may get up to help a neighbour; even an ordinary father usually provides his son with food; even a bad magistrate may listen to a woman in trouble. How much more will God show His love towards a 'sinner'!"
These parables are:
A Householder in Bed (Luke 11. 5-10).
A Son asking for Bread (Luke 11. 11-13).
A Widow and a Magistrate (Luke 18. 1-8).

b. A great banquet (v. 16). A meal such as this was probably in the late afternoon or in the evening, so that it is right to call it a "supper party".

c. All is now ready (v. 17). "Ready" is an important word in this parable.
1. The host was ready to give, and the time came when the meal was ready. So God is ready to give us what we need. He is more ready to give than we are to receive.
2. Some of the guests were ready to eat, some were not. The parable studied in chapter 11 of this book is also about some people who were ready and some who were not.

d. They all alike began to make excuses (v. 18). It may seem strange for anyone to refuse such an invitation. But the Pharisees often refused invitations sent them by Herod, because Herod was a Jew supported by the hated Roman colonial government. And today at United Nations Headquarters representatives of one country sometimes refuse invitations to a party if they are told that a representative of an enemy country is going to be present.
The parables of Jesus are about things that really happen.

e. The householder in anger (v. 21). Readers have sometimes thought that when Jesus told this story of the host's anger He was teaching us about God's anger. But it would be a mistake to say this. This is a story and a parable: it is not an allegory in which each part of the story carries a separate piece of teaching. The anger of the host is just one of the things that make the story complete.
However, it is useful to notice that the word "anger" is used many times in the Bible and is used in three different ways:
1. Human anger which is good and useful. We read of this kind in Eph. 4. 26.
2. Human anger which is sinful: it damages both the angry person and the person against whom it is directed. We read of this in Eph. 4. 31.
3. God's anger, or "wrath". God's anger is God allowing us to suffer because we have refused to take the right way. We experience

His anger whenever we feel the pain which comes from this act of refusal. But God does not lose His temper or take offence.

f. Compel people to come in (v. 23). We have seen that in this story these words mean, "Tell those who are poor and who have not good clothes not to be afraid. Persuade them that they will enjoy the feast when they arrive." Jesus was thinking of those "sinners" and outcasts with whom he often mixed and who were loved by God.

But the words have sometimes been interpreted to mean, "Force people to become Christian." As a result of this wrong interpretation the armies of so-called "Christian nations" have in the past sometimes said to their non-Christian enemies, "We will kill you unless you become Christian." This happened many times in Europe.

In the same way, members of one Church have persecuted the members of another Church because of the same wrong interpretation.

Such a terrible interpretation was made because readers treated the parables as "allegories". They said, "The host is God, the servant is the Church, the people who are invited to the party at the last minute are the non-Christians. Therefore the Church is being commanded to force non-Christians to be baptized."

This shows clearly that it is of great importance to know how to interpret a parable. We cannot say, "Let each person interpret it as he feels." Such terrible mistakes can be avoided if:

a. we read the whole parable instead of picking out a single sentence;

b. we find out when Jesus told the parable and to whom;

c. we compare our interpretation with the teaching of the rest of the New Testament teaching. See Special Note B on p. 67.

STUDY SUGGESTIONS FOR CHAPTER 7

Word Study

1. Human "anger" can be of two kinds, good and bad. What is the difference between the following bad kinds?
   taking offence   losing one's temper

Review of Content

2. Why was the host angry?

3. Why did Jesus tell this story to the Pharisee of whom we read in Luke 14. 1?

4. In what ways were the "poor and maimed and blind" people alike?

5. Why did the host think that the messenger might have to "compel" the last group of guests to come?

6. Why is it unwise for each person to interpret a parable as he feels?
7. What do the following parables tell us about God:
   a. Luke 18. 1-8; *b.* Luke 11. 11-13?

Bible Study

8. Matt. 22. 1-14 seems to contain more parables than the one which St Luke has given us. Which two passages in St Matthew's version are extra to the parable of a Host and his Guests?
9. In what ways is the teaching of Matt. 5. 6 like the teaching of the parable of a Host and his Guests?
10. In what ways were those who came to the supper party like the son who returned home in Luke 15. 11-32?
11. This is a parable about people being "ready" to "accept".
    a. We read in the following verses of people who were "ready". Say in each case what they were ready to do:
       i. Mark 14. 12; ii. John 5. 7; iii. 2 Tim. 4. 6.
    b. Say what gift Christians should "accept" according to:
       i. Mark 4. 20; ii. John 20. 22.

Opinion and Research

12. What special message may Gentiles living in the first century A.D. have found in the parable of a Host and his Guests?
13. In a sermon the preacher said, "This parable teaches us to attend Holy Communion regularly." How far would you agree or disagree with him?
14. "The host did not send away those who were invited at first: they kept themselves away."
    Give an example from everyday life to show that people "keep themselves away" from God's gifts.
15. Look at the picture on p. 62.
    a. What good things do you think the villagers fear to lose if they admit to having tuberculosis?
    b. What could you say to them if you were the visiting doctor?
16. *a.* Do you think it is ever right to be angry?
    b. If so, how do you distinguish between the right kind of anger and the wrong kind?
17. According to St Paul (Acts 20. 35) Jesus said, "It is more blessed to give than to receive." But this parable shows how important it is to receive what God offers.
    a. Are these two sentences contradictory?
    b. How do you interpret them?

SPECIAL NOTE B

Parables and Allegories

I WHAT IS THE DIFFERENCE?

The most important difference between parables and allegories is this: a parable contains one chief lesson; but in an allegory each part of the story gives us a separate lesson.

Two other differences are: (*a*) a parable is usually a short story or saying, an allegory is usually longer; (*b*) a parable is about ordinary events, an allegory often deals with unusual events.

An example of an allegory is the Pilgrim's Progress by John Bunyan. In this story each person teaches us something, and each event has a separate message: the traveller or pilgrim is mankind, the load on his back is his sin, the mud he walks through is his unhappiness, people whom he meets are his temptations or his virtues.

II JESUS TOLD PARABLES
RATHER THAN ALLEGORIES

Two reasons for saying this are:

1. Jesus was a Jew and the Jews made much more use of parables than they did of allegories. There is an allegory in Isaiah 5. 1-7, but there are more parables than allegories in the Old Testament, e.g. the parable of the Poor Man's Lamb (2 Sam. 12. 1-4).

2. Jesus gave His teaching as He travelled round and talked with disciples and strangers. Parables, rather than allegories, are used by those who teach like this. Allegories are longer, and are chiefly used by people who write down their teaching.

But we cannot say that Jesus never used allegories. He probably told the story of the Wicked Vinedressers as an allegory (Mark 12. 1-12). And some people think that Jesus may have told the following as allegories: a Farmer and his Harvest (or the Sower) in Mark 4. 1-20; Weeds in the Wheat (Matt. 13. 24-30); and the Fisherman's Net (Matt. 13. 47-50).

III HIS PARABLES
HAVE OFTEN BEEN TREATED AS ALLEGORIES

Probably they were treated like this soon after He had told them (perhaps when people who were accustomed to using allegories began to join the Church).

Did the writers of the Gospels treat Jesus' parables as allegories? We saw in Special Note A that there is a belief that they did. For example, it is thought that Jesus told a simple parable about a Sower, which we see in Mark 4. 3-8, but that it was later interpreted as an allegory (in vv. 13-20).

It is not certain that this occurred, but the suggestion has to be taken seriously.

However, we do know that for hundreds of years Christians made Jesus' parables into allegories. One example may be given. St Augustine of Hippo interpreted the Parable of the Good Samaritan in this way. He said that the traveller in the story was mankind; Jerusalem was heaven; the Samaritan was Jesus; the thieves were evil spirits; the Priest and Levite were the Jews before the coming of Jesus; the inn was the Church; the inn-keeper was St Paul; the two coins given to him were Baptism and Holy Communion.

There are two things we must say about such an interpretation. First, that it was not Jesus' interpretation. (If He had given such teaching no one who heard it could have understood it. There was no Holy Communion at the time when Jesus told the story.) Secondly, that other preachers who have also made this parable into an allegory have given quite different interpretations of it.

IV   CAN WE TREAT PARABLES AS ALLEGORIES?

1. We can do so if we explain that this way of interpreting a parable is our own way: we shall go wrong if we make it seem that Jesus Himself intended it to be interpreted in this way.

Secondly, our interpretation will be Christian only if it agrees with teaching that is also found in other parts of the New Testament: we shall go wrong if the teaching we take from the parable goes against other teaching of the New Testament.

2. But there are dangers in treating a parable as an allegory, and they are these:

a. We may treat as important a part of the story which Jesus did not intend to be important. The words "compel people to come in" in the parable of the Great Supper are an example of this (Luke 14. 23). Some people who made this parable into an allegory taught that it was right to force people to become Christians (See p. 65, note **f**).

In the same way, if we make the parable of a Householder in Bed (Luke 11. 5-10) into an allegory, we may find that it leads us to wrong ideas about God. In the parable, the man in bed would not listen to his friend until the friend had knocked at his door over and over again. If we pay too much attention to this part of the story, we shall begin to think that God never gives us what we need unless we go on and on begging for it. (See p. 64 for a Note on the interpretation of this parable.)

b. We may make the mistake of thinking that Jesus' teaching is a hidden thing which only clever people can find. Some people have thought this. They have said that Jesus' stories were allegories and that allegories are like rooms which remain locked unless you have the key. If a preacher gives you the key (the interpretation) you can receive Jesus' teaching and eternal life.

Those who say this sometimes quote Matt. 13. 11 to support their opinion. "To you it has been given to know the secrets of the kingdom of heaven, but to them it has not been given."

Two things must be said in reply to this. First that Jesus did not mean that only clever people could understand His teaching. In this verse He was telling them that when He taught, His hearers were divided into two groups. Those who were humble enough to listen to His "secrets" were one group, those who were unwilling to listen were another group. (See Note **b.** on p. 62.) This agrees with Mark 10. 15, "Whoever does not accept the kingdom of God like a child will never enter it" (NEB). Children understand the important things of Jesus' teaching better than many of their elders do.

Secondly, being a Christian is not chiefly getting information about God. It is accepting God's love and loving Him in return. It is following Him and serving Him by serving the people we live with.

c. The most serious danger (as we have seen) is that we may put our own ideas into the parable instead of finding in it the teaching of Jesus. We are always in danger of doing this, but the danger increases when we turn His parables into allegories. The danger becomes much less if we ask: "What was the chief message that Jesus was teaching when He first told this parable?"

.3. If we say that Jesus did not mean most of His parables to be allegories, we may be asked why some of the parables have so many parts. Someone may say, "Surely each part was intended to have a lesson." The answer is that the different parts of the story are there because the story would not be complete without them. In a parable it is not intended that each part shall carry a separate lesson. The parts of a parable are like the parts of a car: the tyres, the wheels, the engine, etc. These parts are all necessary. But a man does not buy a car because he wants wheels, or because tyres are useful things. He buys it so that the whole car, with all its parts together, can take him and other passengers on their journey.

D

STUDY SUGGESTIONS FOR SPECIAL NOTE B

Word Study

1. Say in your own words what an "allegory" is.

Review of Content

2. Are the following true or untrue? Give reasons for your answer in each case.
   a. We know that Jesus never used allegories.
   b. Allegories are usually longer than parables.
   c. We should compare our own interpretation of a parable with the teaching of other parts of the New Testament.
   d. Being a Christian is chiefly getting information about God.

3. What evidence is there that Jesus usually told parables rather than allegories?

4. What evidence is there that St Augustine did not interpret the parable of the Good Samaritan as Jesus Himself interpreted it?

5. Why do some parables have several parts?

6. What steps can we take to discover Jesus' own teaching in a parable, instead of putting our own ideas into it?

Bible Study

7. It is dangerous to treat a parable as an allegory. What false teaching might a reader get if he treated the following verses as parts of allegories?
   a. Luke 11. 7;   b. Luke 14. 23;   c. Matt. 13. 44a.

8. Read 2 Sam. 12. 1-13.
   a. What did Nathan want David to learn through the parable in verses 1-4?
   b. Why do we call this passage a parable?

9. Read Isaiah 5. 1-7.
   a. Why is this story called an allegory?
   b. Who do the following things in the story stand for?
      i. the owner of the vineyard
      ii. the vineyard
      iii. the plants in the vineyard.

Opinion and Research

10. What would you reply to someone who said, "Jesus' teaching is a hidden thing which only clever people can find"?

11. Does any traditional folklore which you know contain allegories? If so, give an example.

Chapter 8.   Travellers on the Road

Luke 10. 30-37
The Parable of the Good Samaritan

I   OUTLINE

A man was travelling down the road that goes from Jerusalem to Jericho when he was attacked by robbers. They took everything he had and nearly killed him.

While he was lying there alone, a Jewish priest who was taking the same road came along. He looked at the man, but walked past him on the other side of the road.

The next traveller was a "Levite", one of those officials who assisted the priests in the Temple. He did the same.

Then came a Samaritan riding a donkey. When he saw the wounded man he went over to him. First he gave him first-aid, using oil and wine, and tearing some cloth to make bandages for the wounds. Then, he put him on the donkey, took him to an inn, and sat with him until the next morning. The Samaritan had to continue his journey then so he gave the innkeeper money and asked him to take care of the wounded man. He promised that if there were any further expenses he would pay them when he travelled that way again.

II   SEEING THE ORIGINAL SITUATION

The situation
St Luke has explained why Jesus told this story. A man came to ask Jesus a question. (He was called a "lawyer", but this means that his work was teaching the Law and Doctrine of God as it is found in the Old Testament. He was a leader among the Jews.) It seems that he had been either troubled or interested by the things that Jesus was doing and saying. So he put a test to Jesus by saying, "What do you think we must do in order to have eternal life?"

Instead of replying, Jesus asked, "What does God's Law say?" The man recited two verses from the Old Testament: "Love God", "Love your neighbour." "Yes," said Jesus, "the way to have eternal life is indeed to *love*."

But the man wanted to show that he was serious in his questioning, and said, "Yes. But it is hard to know who your neighbour is." It was then that Jesus told this story about three Jews and a Samaritan.

When the story was finished, Jesus asked the "lawyer" another question: "Who do you think was neighbour to the wounded man?" This was a really hard question to answer. The lawyer was in the habit of saying that Jews were neighbours to Jews. We know from John 4. 9 that Jews and Samaritans were such bitter enemies that they did not even speak to each other. But after hearing this story he had to say that the Samaritan was behaving like a neighbour to the wounded man. "Yes," said Jesus, "and this is what you yourself must do if you want eternal life."

So in answer to the lawyer's question, Jesus was giving teaching about the character of His followers. He was saying:
"My true followers, i.e. those who are being given 'eternal life', are those who show love above everything else."

In this parable, therefore, Jesus was rebuking the Jewish religious leaders. He rebuked them because they gave much attention to serving God by attending public worship and by obeying each part of the Law, but they gave too little attention to serving Him by serving their fellow human beings. It was not only a rebuke: He was calling on them with gentleness to change their ways (e.g. when He said to the lawyer, "You do this, too.").

Suggested Application
Jesus, however, was not only saying, "My followers ought to be more loving." There is special teaching about loving behind this parable.

1. Love those human beings who are in need.

We have seen in the parable of the Lost Sheep and other parables, that this is how God loves.

First, this means that we are not to show love only to those who belong to our own family or clan or town or nation or race. In these days there are many divisions between men, and this teaching is especially needed. We think of the divisions between Arabs and Jews, between groups of Negroes in the U.S.A. and certain groups of "whites", between Sikhs and Hindus in some parts of India, and many other divisions which are less well-known. We think also of those who show love across those divisions. Recently, the writer of this book saw a Chinese from Mauritius collecting money for the blind people of London outside a London station. On the same day the radio told of a feast which was being given to the orphaned English children of Birmingham by the Jamaican Club of that city.

There is a story which comes from a part of Asia where many people had cholera. Some American doctors and nurses were treating patients. There was one boy there who was in very great pain. One of the Americans said, "See how much he suffers." Another of them said, "See how much these people suffer." A third said, "See how much we suffer." The first two men were kind, but looked at the boy as if he was apart from them. It was as if they were on one side of a wall and the boy was on the other. The third said, "We", and he meant, "We human beings, we mankind, we people all on the same side of the wall". So he spoke with greater truth and love.

Secondly, we are not to show love only to those who are good. Yet religious people do often make the mistake of refusing help to those whose lives are not good. A crowd of people coming out of an evening service in a Christian church passed a girl who was drunk and staggering about the street. Some seemed to be afraid of her, some seemed angry, some seemed as if they felt they were superior to her. But there was one woman who said to the girl, "Where do you live, dear? I'll take you home."

2. You cannot love God unless you love people.

Even though people believe in God they are sometimes tempted to think that they can love and serve God without loving and serving people on earth. Amos told the Jews of his day that they spent much time worshipping God but forgot to treat poor people with justice. "God hates this worship", he said. (See Amos 5. 21-24.)

In St John's Epistle this is said several times: "If a man does not love the brother whom he has seen, it cannot be that he loves God whom he has not seen" (1 John 4. 20, NEB).

The parable of the Sheep and Goats shows this also. In this story, the Son of Man said, "When I was hungry, you gave me food . . . ." They replied, "When did we do that?", and He said, "Anything you did for one of my brothers here, however humble, you did for me" (Matt. 25. 40, NEB).

Perhaps the officials of the Church are specially tempted to forget this. The parable of Travellers on the Road certainly shows this. A Christian priest may want to show love to God by conducting the services reverently and preaching well. Yet if he refuses to speak to a man who has done him some injury, it is not only that man whom he is failing to love. He is failing to love God. A Christian teacher in a school may be careful to say his prayers every morning before he leaves home, but if he despises the weak pupils in his class, it is God whom he is failing to love.

3. You know a truth when you *do* it.

The lawyer learnt from Jesus that the way to have eternal life is by loving. Then Jesus added, "That is the right answer. Now *do* that and you will live" (v. 28). According to Jesus, we do not know a truth until we do it. We do not know it until we live by it and act upon it. (See John 3. 21.) This is true concerning all the teaching given by Jesus, including the teaching about Himself. Some people once asked Him, "How can we tell if your teaching is true or not?" Jesus' reply was, "If you are willing to *do* it, you will find out if it is true." (See John 7. 15-17.)

Sometimes a person says, "I must first know who Jesus was before I work for Him. I must first understand how He could be both man and God." But it is by actively serving our fellow human beings that we find out who Jesus is. We remember Matt. 25. 40, "Anything you did for one of my brothers . . . you did for *me.*" Thinking and doing must go together.

4. What matters most is that mercy should be done: it is less important who does it.

The parable shows this clearly.

Today the State is doing many of the acts of mercy which the Church used to do, e.g. most hospitals used to be Church hospitals, but are no longer so. There have been Christians who said, "There are now only a few ways in which we Christians can show mercy." But this is a mistake. If a Christian is a dispenser or cleaner or nurse or secretary in a State hospital, he is helping to bring the healing power of God to people in need. This is his true Christian service, it is his "Church work", so long as he is doing it in love and mercy. And there is perhaps a man who never worships God working beside him. This man also serves God if he works with love and care.

5. We are judged by what we have done and by what we have failed to do.

The priest and Levite did not think they had done any wrong. And it is true that they did not steal from the wounded man or harm him in any way. But they failed to take care of him, and this was as bad as crime.

Sometimes we examine ourselves and say, "What wrong have I done today?", and this is a good practice. But we must also ask, "Were there people whom I could have helped today, but failed to help? Was there a word of encouragement which I could have spoken but did not?"

6. People who love and give.

In this story the Samaritan showed his love and care by the way in which he gave. But we should notice two further truths about the way in which we love and give.

a. It is possible to give but to give without loving. One country may give ten million pounds to another country, but the chief reason may be to persuade that country to buy certain manufactured goods. A woman visits her neighbours when they are ill, but her chief reason may be to receive praise. (She may be quite ignorant that this is her chief reason.)

b. We show our love also by the way in which we receive. Someone apologizes to me for an injury he has done me and I need to love him in order to accept his apology. Someone criticizes what I have said and I need to love him in order to receive the criticism.

III SEEING OUR OWN SITUATION

1. When we read this parable, we cannot simply say that the priest and Levite did badly and that the Samaritan did well. We say, "These three people are myself. Many times a day I become either the priest and Levite, or the Samaritan. Each of these times God gives me a choice. If I make the right choice, then I am sharing in the kind of life which is most worth living (the life which is called "eternal").

Every reader can supply examples of these times. Here are a few examples which the parable itself suggests:

As Christians we belong to a village Church, and hear that one member has resigned after a quarrel with the minister and some of the congregation. He has joined a small sect in a nearby town. Now the man's wife is ill. Some of the congregation are so angry with the man that they will not go inside his house. Others want to help her. We can choose which we shall do.

We read in a newspaper that refugees from another country are coming to our district. On the same page of the newspaper we read that more than half of the people of the world have too little to eat. Part of us says, "There is so much suffering that it is useless to do anything to help these refugees." Part of us says, "We can at least give hospitality to one family."

In a certain country two groups of people each claim that a district belongs to them by tradition. There is deep hatred between them over the matter. We belong to one group and we hear that the leader of the other group has been accused of bribery by the government. We know that he is innocent, and that it is another person who is to blame. We can keep silent. Or we can give evidence.

A woman is walking along a street in a big city, when a man snatches the bag out of her hand. All her money is in the bag. The street is full of people, and they see what has happened. They know that the man will escape if they do not stop him; they also know that there is danger in stopping him. We are in that crowd: do we try to stop him? Or do we stand still?

In each case someone chooses to share in the kind of life that is most worth living *or* decides not to share in it.

NOTES

a. From Jerusalem to Jericho (v. 30). Jerusalem is 2300 feet above sea level, Jericho is 1300 feet below sea level, so the road goes down hill all the way. It is 20 miles long and goes through deserted country. It was thus easy for robbers to hide behind rocks or round a corner.

When the author of this book was living in Jerusalem, there was a famous robber called Abu Jildeh. He stopped 24 cars at one place on this road, and robbed the passengers of all their money and watches. He said he would cut off one woman's finger if she could not get the ring off her finger and give it to him.

b. He passed by (v. 31). Probably the priest passed by because it was extremely dangerous to remain in a place where there were robbers. Having robbed and wounded one man, they might still be waiting for the next person to rob.

But there may have been another reason why he passed by. We know from Numbers 19. 11-13 that, according to Jewish law, anyone who touched a dead body was "unclean" for seven days. During that time he could take no part in religious services. It was the work of the priests to conduct these services and the Levites assisted them. So each one may have said, "I must put first the worship of God", and so kept away from the wounded man. But neither of them even went to see if the man was alive or dead. (And we have seen that the worship of God and the service of men cannot be separated in this way.)

c. Samaritan (v. 33). The Samaritans were a nation who had been the enemies of the Jews for a long time. They were hated by the Jews chiefly because their ancestors had come from the marriages of Jewish and non-Jewish parents. A few years before Jesus told this parable Samaritans had put a dead man's bones in the court of the Temple during the Passover Festival, and the Jews' hatred had increased.

Some people say that the "Samaritan" in the parable did not belong to this nation, because Samaritans never visited Jerusalem. They say that he was a Jew who did not keep the Law and that such people were sometimes given the name of "Samaritan". Jesus Himself was called "Samaritan" for this reason (John 8. 48).

But whichever interpretation is given, the man was someone from whom the Jews were cut off.

d. Came to where he was (v. 33). Readers have found that these words remind them of still further teaching about Christian love:

1. The Samaritan did this at a risk to himself. So also a nurse takes a risk when she looks after someone with an infectious disease. And people who try to help prostitutes run a risk when they make it possible for them to begin a different sort of life: they themselves are sometimes misunderstood and are accused of being "immoral".

2. He did it although others were not doing it.

3. He did it although he had not expected to meet the wounded man. Christians are ready to serve other people in unexpected ways: they are ready to help people they have not chosen to help.

e. Two denarii (v. 35). (See note **d** on p. 48.)

"The true followers of Jesus are those who show love above everything else . . .
The Samaritan did this at a risk to himself."

A group of students were trapped by rising water in dangerous caves in northern
England. Volunteers risked their lives for 56 hours before Joan Smith, the last to
be saved, was brought to the surface.

f. Which of these three, do you think, proved neighbour (v. 36). This question by Jesus shows the way in which He did most of His teaching. It was not His custom to deliver lectures or to give answers to His listeners' questions. He used to tell a story and then say, "What do *you* think?" He did this because the lessons which we are helped to discover for ourselves are the lessons which make a difference to our lives. He did it because He wants us to co-operate with Him.

Another parable which He used in this way is the story about Two Debtors (Luke 7. 41, 42). At the end of that story, Jesus said, "Which of these two men do you think will love him more?"

STUDY SUGGESTIONS FOR CHAPTER 8

Word Study

1. Jesus told this parable to a "lawyer". What was the work of a "lawyer" in those days?

2. *a.* What do people usually mean today when they use the word "neighbour"?
   b. What did the lawyer mean by it in Luke 10. 27?
   c. What did Jesus mean by it in Luke 10. 36?

3. *a.* What does "taking a risk" mean?
   b. Give an example of someone "taking a risk" for a good reason.

4. Jesus said that someone who knew how to love would "live". Choose *two* out of the following phrases to show what Jesus meant by the word "live" in Luke 10. 28.
   to breathe
   to live fully and abundantly on this earth
   to escape the death of the body
   to live fully on this earth and after death.
   (You may find it useful to read the following verses before answering the question: John 5. 24; John 10. 10; John 11. 25.)

Review of Content

5. When the Samaritan saw the wounded man what did he
   a. feel? *b.* do?

6. Who was Jesus rebuking when He told this parable, and why was He rebuking them?

7. Some people asked Jesus how they could tell whether His teaching was true. What did He say in reply?

8. When we examine our own behaviour, it is not enough to ask ourselves "What wrong have I done?" What else is needed?

9. Why did the robbers choose the Jerusalem-Jericho road for their attacks?

10. Give two reasons why the priest and the Levite did not stop to help the wounded man.

Bible Study

11. When Jesus had told the story of Travellers on the Road, He asked a question. Read the following passages from St Luke's Gospel, and say in each case why you think Jesus asked a question.
   a. 6. 9;   *b.* 7.42;   *c.* 10. 36;   *d.* 14. 5;   *e.* 18. 41.

12. What do the following passages tell us about "loving"?
   a. Amos 5. 21-24;   *b.* Matt. 25. 31-40.

13. Choose *three* words or phrases from 1 Cor. 13. 4-7 which describe the behaviour of the Samaritan in this parable. Give reasons for your choice in each case.

Opinion and Research

14. Imagine that you are the drunken girl mentioned in this chapter (p. 73) and write the story from your point of view.

15. Name two groups of people in your country between whom there is distrust and division.
   a. Why does this distrust exist?
   b. What is being done, or could be done, to create trust between them?

16. *a.* How many Samaritans are there living today?
   b. Where do they live now?

17. This chapter contains examples of choosing whether to give help or not. Give two more examples from your own experience.

18. Name two ways in which the Church in your opinion is responsible for caring for people in need. Say in each case:
   a. when this work began;
   b. who were the leaders of this work.

Chapter 9. A Farmer and his Treasure and a Trader and his Business

Matt. 13. 44-46
The Parables of the Hidden Treasure and of the Pearl of Great Price

I OUTLINE

A farmer was ploughing his field, when suddenly the plough hit a hard object. He dug down with his hoe, and discovered, to his delight, that it was a box full of gold. He buried it again quickly before anyone else could see what he was doing, and marked the place with a stick.

At the end of the day he went home. The land did not belong to him, so he knew he would have to buy the field in order to get the treasure. He could not do this without selling everything that he possessed. But the value of the treasure was clearly greater than the value of his possessions, and he decided to sell everything he had.

The next day he sold his possessions, to the surprise of his neighbours. Then he told the landlord that he wanted to buy the field. The landlord was surprised, too, but he agreed to sell it. The farmer paid the price that was asked, and ran back to the field, and dug up his treasure.

————————

Alongside this story of the farmer, we are given one which is like it, about a trader and his business.

There was a trader who spent his life buying pearls and selling them at a profit. One day he was offered one which he could see was very specially valuable. The owner did not seem to know how valuable it was. But even so the trader could not pay the price.

He went home and thought about this pearl. Then he decided that it was to his advantage to buy it, even if he had to sell all his possessions in order to do so. And that is what he did. He sold everything he had, and so became the owner of the precious pearl.

II SEEING THE ORIGINAL SITUATION

The situation
These parables seem to have been told at a time when Jesus was gathering new followers round Him. Probably this was in the early part of His ministry. There were very many people who heard His teaching and had to decide if they would join Him or not. They knew that if they did join Him, it would mean that there would be big changes in their lives. Was it wise to follow Him, or foolish? We read of one of these people in Mark 10. 17-30.

In these two parables Jesus was helping such people to make their decision. He was saying:

"If you decide to follow me, you will gain more than you will lose. I promise you the best kind of life which anyone can live."

Suggested Application

1. The life that we are offered by God is real treasure.

We have already seen this in the parable of a Host and his Guests. Being a Christian is not chiefly trying to keep rules, but it is enjoying the best kind of life.

Different writers use different words to describe this life. For example, in John 10. 10 it is called "life in all its fullness" (NEB), in John 3. 16, "eternal life". In the Beatitudes (Matt. 5. 3-11) it is called being "blessed". St Paul calls it "salvation" and being "in Christ". In each of these passages it is the same life that is being described.

In this kind of life we know that we belong to God, through Jesus Christ. We know that we are accepted by Him in spite of our faults. It is a life in which we share both the happiness and sufferings of other people. There is both pain and joy. It is a full life.

The special teaching of these two parables is that this life is joyfully received. V. 44 says, "in his joy".

2. This life can be lived now.

When Jesus offered this life to people, He taught that they could have it now, and in this world. "If you believe in me, you *have already* eternal life." (See John 6. 47.) These parables remind us of this.

It is, like the treasure, not very far below the surface of the ground. It is not out of reach. (See Acts 17. 27, "He is not far from each one of us.")

It is found during our ordinary day's work and life.

But we often forget this. Two schoolboys were studying at home in preparation for examinations. In the same room was the grandfather of one of them, reading his Bible. One of the boys asked, "What is your grandfather doing?" The other laughed and said, "He's like us; he's preparing for his finals." (He meant that his grandfather was reading his Bible to prepare for the time when God would examine him, after his death.) But if we think that the words of Jesus are only to prepare us for life after death we shall make a big mistake; we shall fail to make the best of the gifts God has given us in this life.

3. It is worth making any sacrifice in order to have this life.

We may be surprised to hear Jesus talking as if religion were a trade or a business. But it was Jesus who said, "What will your profit be?" (See Mark 8. 36.) The pearl-trader asked, "Will I make a profit if I sell my possessions and get this pearl?" He decided that he would make a profit; and so he sold all he had. It is right for us to talk like this about eternal life.

But what do we human beings have which we can sell? What does it cost us? What is the price of the best kind of life?

What we pay is our whole life as it is lived apart from God. Another way to express it is to say that we give up our independence: we do this in order to be ruled by God. (We saw that the Prodigal Son returned home when he stopped saying, "I want my way", i.e. when he was willing to give up being completely independent of his family.) This is the teaching of Mark 8. 35, "If a man will let himself be lost for my sake and for the Gospel, that man is safe" (NEB). (See also Phil. 3. 8: "I have suffered the loss of all things . . . in order that I may gain Christ.")

This "payment" of the whole of our lives which are lived apart from God must come first. And when we make this payment, we find that there are also certain other habits or things which we must give up too. One man decided that he must give up his present job because it prevented him from looking after his family. A second man gave up cigarettes. A girl gave up a rich man whom she did not really love and married a poor man whom she did love. Another girl gave up her body to be killed in a civil war so that the rest of her family might be saved; she did this as her offering to God.

There is no rule or regulation. Each one finds out what it is necessary to give.

Someone may say that God gives us eternal life freely and that no one can buy it. This is indeed true. In Matt. 10. 8 Jesus says, "You received without cost" (NEB). But even gifts have to be received at the cost of something. Two children are playing outside their house. Their mother calls out, "Come in and have your supper." The supper is free, but until they give up their play they will not be able to receive it and enjoy it.

III SEEING OUR OWN SITUATION

Many times during our lives we are like that farmer and that pearl-trader, because throughout our lives God offers us opportunities to have a fuller life at a cost.

A boy's parents saved up enough money to send him to a secondary school which was far from his home. The boy saw that he was being offered something good, but he also saw that certain things would have to be given up if he accepted it. He would have to give up his dependence on his mother and the comfort of his home. He would have to give up these things in order to grow up and become the man that he was able to become.

"Throughout our lives God offers us opportunities to have a fuller life at a cost."

These Tanzanian children were happy to spend time carrying timber to build a new school for their village. They knew that learning to read and write would help them to get better jobs in the future.

Jesus gave the example of the mother who is willing to suffer labour pains because she will have the joy of bringing a human being into the world (John 16. 21).

There was a man who had been born blind. His family looked after him well and the neighbours were kind to him. But no doctor could make him see. When he was about thirty he was taken to a new doctor, who said, "I think that I can help you to see." The blind man was at first terribly afraid. He thought to himself, "I know the life of a blind man: but it will be a strange life if I begin to see. I shall have to meet strange people; I shall have to be trained for work; my family will no longer look after me as they do now." As he had never used his eyes, he could not know what pleasure he would have if he could see. But he had a friend who understood his fears. This friend said, "It is for you to decide. All I can do is to assure you that, if you have the courage to go to this doctor, your life will be fuller and richer."

When St Augustine of Hippo was a young man, he looked everywhere for a life that was full and joyful. At one time he looked for it in drunkenness and wild behaviour with women. When he had discovered that the Christian life was the fullest and most joyful life, he wrote, "The life that I was once afraid to give up I now gave up with joy, because You, Lord, put it away from me. You are the true and greatest Joy."

A man who has been treated badly by many people protects himself by distrusting everyone he meets. He is unsociable, so he has no friends. But then he does meet a group of people who are both good and friendly; and each time he meets them he is given an opportunity to trust them and to gain friends. But he has to decide. Will he give up his old way of protecting himself in order to have this new way of living? Or will he not have enough faith and courage?

It is in these ways that we find "eternal life"; because in each case the treasure that is offered is a part of the full and eternal life which God wants us to enjoy.

NOTES

a. A man found (v. 44). In this parable the farmer found his treasure although he was not looking for it. In the other parable the trader found it by searching. Human beings seem to find eternal life in different ways. It seems that it is given to some who have not been looking for it; it comes on them by surprise. Others find it after long years of searching.

b. Covered up (v. 44). This seems to be a dishonest thing to do. The farmer covered up the treasure so that the landlord would sell him the land as ordinary agricultural land. If he had known that it contained a treasure, he would not have sold it to the farmer.

If Jesus had told this parable in order that we might imitate the farmer, we should be troubled at his teaching. But this was not Jesus' aim. This is not an allegory in which each part of the story contains some teaching. Jesus told the story with one chief lesson in His mind: "The life I offer you is worth the cost." (See Special Note B, p. 67.)

c. The kingdom of heaven is like a merchant (v. 45). When Jesus used the words "Kingdom of Heaven" He did not think of a place. He thought of the rule or "Kingship" or "supremacy" which God has over His people. God is truly supreme, although many do not accept His rule or accept its benefits. (See note c. on p. 48.)

What two things are being compared in this parable? Clearly Jesus was not comparing God or the Kingdom of Heaven (i.e. God's supremacy) to a merchant. He was comparing the way that someone accepts God's supremacy to the way that the merchant behaved. The NEB translation is clearer than the RSV here: "Here is another picture of the Kingdom of Heaven . . . ."

There are many parables which begin with the words: "The Kingdom of Heaven is like . . .", e.g. Matt. 13. vv. 24; 31; 33; 47; and Matt. 18. 23; 20. 1. 22. 2; 25. 1. We should interpret them in the same way in which we have interpreted Matt. 13. vv. 44 and 45.

d. In search of fine pearls (v. 45). In those days this work was done by a great many people. They travelled to countries where the best pearls were to be found in the sea, e.g. to the Persian Gulf, India, and Britain.

STUDY SUGGESTIONS FOR CHAPTER 9

Word Study

1. What does "Kingdom of Heaven" mean?

2. The word "joy" is used in v. 44.
   a. What gave the farmer joy?
   b. These are some of the statements which the Bible contains about the joy of a believer:
      i. It is the result of a right relationship with God.
      ii. It is given by God's Holy Spirit.
      iii. Even suffering cannot destroy it.
   Say which of the following verses expresses each statement most closely: Psalm 16. 11; Acts 5. 41; Gal. 5. 22.

Review of Content

3. *a.* In what ways are the two parables we have studied in this chapter alike?
   b. Describe two ways in which they are different.

4. What did the following people (i) give up? (ii) find?
   a. The boy mentioned in the chapter who went far away to school.
   b. The mother mentioned in John 16. 21.
   c. The blind man who went to a new doctor.

5. a. Why did the farmer mentioned in Matt. 13. 14 cover up the treasure that he had found?
   b. What would you reply to someone who said that this was a dishonest act and that Jesus was thus encouraging dishonesty?

6. a. What does it cost us to obtain eternal life?
   b. What would you reply to someone who said, "There is no 'cost' because eternal life is a free gift from God"?

Bible Study

7. Several different words or phrases are used in the New Testament to describe the life that God offers us. Which words or phrases in each of the following verses are used to describe this life? Matt. 5. 8; Matt. 19. 29; Acts 16. 17; Rom. 7. 6; Rom. 8. 1; Gal. 2. 19; Titus 3. 7.

8. a. In what ways is the story told in Mark 10. 17-22 like the two parables studied in this chapter?
   b. In what ways is it different?

9. "Jesus was not comparing God or the Kingdom of Heaven (i.e. God's supremacy) to a merchant. He was comparing the way that someone accepts God's supremacy to the way in which a merchant behaved." Remembering this, complete the following sentences:
   a. In Matt. 13. 44 the way that a man accepts God's supremacy is compared to the way . . . .
   b. In Matt. 13. 47-50 the way that God judges mankind is compared to the way . . . .

Opinion and Research

10. What would you reply to someone who read the words "sold all that he had", and said, "Christians are always being told to give up what they enjoy: that is why there are so few of them"?

11. Write a parable of your own which could bring people of today the same message which these two parables bring.

12. A great Christian, Friedrich von Hügel, once described how he met an older man who gave him much help: "When I first met him I met a life that was so rich and deep and full that it made mine seem thin . . . Then I saw that his life had become like this at a cost, at the cost of . . . his own self-will so that God's will could be done in him. I was looking at something costly and I wanted it!" In what way was von Hügel's attitude like that of the Farmer and the Trader in these parables?

Chapter 10.   A Rich Man and his Debtor

Matt. 18. 23-35
The Parable of the Unforgiving Debtor

I   OUTLINE

There was a king who employed State officials to collect the taxes, and to control the finances of his kingdom in other ways. At certain times he used to inspect their accounts.

On one of these inspections he found that one of the officials owed him millions of pounds. (Perhaps this man had been borrowing tax money for a long time and was unable to pay it back.) The amount was so large that there was no way in which the official could pay it. So the king ordered that the man and his family and his possessions should be sold.

Then the official begged to be given time to pay. The king knew that the man could never pay. But out of his generosity he made him a present of the whole amount, and the official was free of his debt.

When he had left the palace, this man happened to meet a junior official who owed him a few pounds. He immediately became very angry and took hold of him by the throat, and said, "You scoundrel, why don't you pay your debt?" The junior begged to be given time to pay. But the first man had him put in prison until he or his relations should pay the debt.

Other government officials saw what happened and they reported it to the king. The king sent for the man who had been let off his huge debt, and said, "I was sorry for you and let you off your debt. Yet you treat this junior without pity. I cannot overlook this. I sentence you to imprisonment with severe punishment."

II   SEEING THE ORIGINAL SITUATION

The situation
According to St Matthew Jesus told this story because of a question that St Peter had asked.

Peter came to Jesus and said, "We have noticed that you forgive people who injure you, and you have told us to do the same. I think that we should not only forgive people once, but even seven times. Is that a good rule?" Jesus said, "If you want to count the number of times you should forgive, then count up to seventy times seven before you stop forgiving. But people who really forgive do not do so according to a rule, nor by counting or measuring." Then He told them this story.

Here, then, is another story in which Jesus described the character

of His followers. It does not only show us what forgiveness is. The chief thing that Jesus was saying is this:
"*My disciples offer to other people the same love and forgiveness which they have received from God.*"

Suggested Application
1. What is forgiveness, that is, the forgiveness which is offered by God to man and the forgiveness which one man offers to another man?

Forgiveness is treating someone better than he deserves. (The official in the story did not deserve to be excused his enormous debt.) God treats us like this, and we call it His "grace".

Forgiveness is giving without a limit. (The king made a present of the whole amount of his debt to the official.) So God does not say, "I will forgive adultery, but I cannot forgive deeds done in anger." He wonderfully says, "Come to me *all* who have heavy loads." We learn in John 3. 34 that when God gives His spirit He does not measure it out. In the same way, a wife who forgives her husband will not say to him, "You were rude to me twice this morning and you forgot three things yesterday. But I am willing to forgive five offences." No one who spoke like that would be offering forgiveness "from the heart" (v. 35).

Forgiveness is offered in order that fellowship may exist. God forgives us because He is concerned with us as people. He wants to restore the fellowship between Himself and ourselves. So a wife who forgives her husband from the heart does so because the fellowship between them matters to her very much indeed.

Forgiveness is costly. Someone has to bear the cost of forgiveness. In the story the king bore the whole cost. We say that God forgave mankind through the death of Jesus. But Jesus was His own and only Son. That was part of the cost of forgiveness and God bore it. There was a young teacher who did his work well but was not liked by his headmaster. Each time he applied for promotion the headmaster prevented it by writing unfair letters about him. The teacher was able to go on forgiving that headmaster and to work without quarrelling with him. But those unfair letters were like a load of pain and it was he who had to carry that load. He had to be strong to carry it. It is strong people who forgive.

2. Accepting forgiveness from God.

In this parable the official accepted forgiveness from the king without difficulty. "Of course he did," we say, "he gained something by doing so. If he had not, he would have been in prison."

When God offers us forgiveness we shall only be able to accept it if we can see that we shall gain by doing so. Often we do not see this. Often we do not accept it even when we have asked for it. Why is this?

It may be because we feel like this: "If God forgives me and accepts me, I shall be expected to live as He wants. I could not do that. I should fail too often. It is easier to remain as I am." A school-teacher noticed that one girl in her class often failed to answer questions although she seemed to know the answers. One day she asked the girl about this, and the girl said, "If I were too successful I should be high in the class list, and I am afraid that I might not be able to stay there." Often we too are afraid, afraid to be forgiven. We cannot believe that God will go on forgiving each time we fail.

Yet what God offers is even more precious than what the king gave the official. The king forgave the man his debt: God offers us a personal relationship, a friendship, a fellowship such as the one which the father gave to his son in Luke 15. 20.

3. Accepting forgiveness from God cannot be separated from offering forgiveness to other people.

As we have seen, this is the central teaching of the parable. If we refuse to forgive other people, we make ourselves unable to receive God's forgiveness. Our dealings with other people and our dealings with God then become like oil and water: you can put them together in a bottle and shake them up, but they will not mix. The oil goes to the top: the water sinks to the bottom. We are behaving without love, and God is treating us with love: the two do not mix.

The official in the story made this mistake. He was glad that the king treated him better than he deserved and not according to the law. But he told the other man that he deserved to be put in prison according to the law.

God does not say, "If I see anyone who is not forgiving others, I shall be very angry and I shall refuse to forgive him." He says, "I offer you all forgiveness. But you cannot receive it unless you also forgive." Similarly, a lecturer may speak in French, but if we have never learnt that language we cannot receive what he says.

So Jesus was not giving us a rule to keep by telling the parable. He was not saying, "You ought to forgive each other." He was saying again what He said in Matt. 5. 7, "It is people who show mercy who are able to receive mercy." See also the words in Matt. 6. 12, "Forgive us our debts, as we also have forgiven our debtors." See also Matt. 5. 44, 45; 7. 1; 10. 8b; Luke 6. 36; Eph. 4. 32: "Forgiving one another, as God in Christ forgave you."

4. None of our dealings with God can be separated from our dealings with people.

In the story the official who was excused his huge debt kept his dealings with the king separate from his own dealings with the junior official. But the king told him that this was not possible.

It is easy to make the same mistake. We think we can love God and

"If we forgive as we have been forgiven, we experience a peace that is God's gift . . . If we do not, we experience the pain of separation."

These two schoolboys have just had a fight. But now that they are friends again, the joy of reconciliation is clearly stronger than the pain of having quarrelled.

say our prayers and meet Him in His Church. But we are less careful about our treatment of the people around us. But Jesus says that it is impossible to separate the two. If we think that we can love God greatly and love people less, we are deceiving ourselves. In such a case, it is not God whom we are loving greatly. It is a figure whom we have made in our own minds and whom we are calling "God". Someone who loves God as He really is loves people with exactly the same strength. We learnt this from the parables of Travellers on the Road (Chapter 8), and the Sheep and Goats (Matt. 25. 31-46).

5. The results of forgiving and not forgiving.

If we forgive as we have been forgiven, we experience a peace which is God's gift. A husband and wife said recently that the happiest times of their life together were the times when they forgave each other after there had been bitterness between them.

If we do not forgive other people, we lose this peace. We experience the pain of being separated. This is a kind of "torture", such as the official experienced (v. 34, NEB).

III SEEING OUR OWN SITUATION

1. As we read this story again, we are bound to feel angry again at the cruelty of the official who had been let off his debt. But perhaps we also feel afraid as we read it and ask, "Am I that man?"

We are indeed often in the same situation, and we behave as the cruel official did. We know that God in His generosity has forgiven us, and yet we find it hard to forgive people who have injured us. This is happening all the time. Here are some examples:

"My elder brother whom I greatly admired has now run away from home with another man's wife. How can I forgive him?"

"I quarrelled with a man working in the same place as I work, and have apologized. But he will not accept my apology and is telling other people about my 'rudeness'."

"My wife has been late cooking the supper for several days."

"My Church committee have found out that it was boys who broke the windows in the church so they want to close the Boys' Club."

"My country has been at war with another country and we cannot forget the cruelty that we experienced."

Jesus taught that our behaviour in these situations can be changed. It is possible to forgive and to go on forgiving. When we are injured by someone the pain may remain with us for a time even though we have forgiven him. But the bitterness can be taken away and we do not have to remain separated from those who did the injury.

2. If we want to go further and to ask *how* we can learn to forgive, the parable helps us to answer this:

a. By remembering that we ourselves have been forgiven very much by God; by seeing that God has already forgiven us more than we have to forgive others. If we could think of all the wrong things we have done and all the good deeds we have failed to do, and if we could think of all the ways in which we have shared in the wrong-doings of our family and nation, then the wrong done to us would seem much smaller than we thought it was.

b. By knowing that God has forgiven us completely. It is guilty people who find it most hard to forgive. When there is a part of me which I do not believe God has forgiven, then I am ashamed of that part of me. Perhaps I have been dishonest and have never told God about it or asked for His forgiveness. This guilt is painful, and I hide it deep in my mind. But when I see the dishonesty of other people, a part of me remembers my own dishonesty with shame, and I say, "I cannot forgive dishonesty." This is what Jesus meant when He said, "You look at the speck of sawdust in your brother's eye, with never a thought for the great plank in your own." (Matt. 7. 3-5, NEB.)

NOTES

a. Other "Parables of Discipleship". This parable is one of those which answers such questions as "What sort of life does a disciple of Jesus live?", or "How can I obtain eternal life?", or "What makes my life full and complete?", or "What sort of person did God intend me to be?"

Other parables which are probably of this kind are:

Travellers on the Road (Luke 10. 30-37. See Chapter 8).

A Farmer and his Treasure (Matt. 13. 44. See Chapter 9).

A Trader and his Business (Matt. 13. 45, 46. See Chapter 9).

A Builder (Luke 14. 28-30), and a King Going to War (Luke 14. 31, 32). "A disciple serves his Lord at cost to himself."

A Farmer and his Labourer (Luke 17. 7-10). "There is no limit to the devotion and service which a disciple offers to his Lord."

Salt in the Food, and a City on a Hill, and a Lamp on a Lampstand (Matt. 5. 13-16). "A disciple shares the things which are most precious to him."

The Speck and the Plank (Matt. 7. 3-5). "A disciple lives in fellowship with others by being willing to know himself." Perhaps the parable of Seats at Table (Luke 14. 7-11) also carries this message.

b. A king who wished to settle accounts (v. 23). Jesus often says that God is like someone who wants to settle accounts with us. And we are expected to give account to Him for the way in which we live. (We think of the parable of a Householder and his Servants, Matt. 25. 14-30, the parable of a Clever Agent, Luke 16. 1-9, and the parable of a Servant left in Charge, Luke 12. 42-46.)

c. In anger his lord delivered him (v. 34). Since this is a parable and not an allegory, we do not say that the king in the story is God, because: (i) God does not change His mind as this king did; (ii) God does not suddenly become angry, like the king, and say, "If you will not forgive, then I will not forgive you."

STUDY SUGGESTIONS FOR CHAPTER 10

Word Study

1. The words "forgiving" and "forgetting" are used in this chapter. Give examples from everyday life to show the difference in meaning between them.

2. In what way is "forgiveness" like "grace"?

3. Give another English word which means "forgive".

4. Which *five* of the following words stand for personal relationships?
   friendship   hardship   sonship   leadership
   fellowship   worship   scholarship

Review of Content

5. What special teaching did Jesus want His hearers to learn through the parable of a Rich Man and his Debtor?

6. What did the king do when it was discovered that the official owed him a huge sum of money?

7. What did Jesus mean when He told Peter to forgive people 490 times?

8. What is the object or purpose of forgiving?

9. What does the behaviour of the young teacher who was disliked by his headmaster show us about "forgiveness"?

10. Are the following true or untrue? Give reasons for your answer in each case.
   a. God refuses to forgive anyone who refuses to forgive other people.
   b. Jesus laid down a law that we must forgive each other.
   c. The king in the parable stands for God.

11. What were the results of being forgiven for:
   a. the forgiven son in Luke 15. 11-32?
   b. the forgiven official in the parable of a Rich Man and his Debtor?

Bible Study

12. What sentence in the Lord's Prayer is like the teaching of the parable of a Rich Man and his Debtor?

93

13. Read the following parables and say in each case:
    a. what special teaching Jesus wanted His hearers to learn;
    b. which words in each parable point to that teaching:
    Luke 17. 7-10;   Matt. 5. 15.

14. In what ways is the teaching of the following passages like the teaching of the parable of a Rich Man and his Debtor?
    a. Matt. 10. 8b;   b. Matt. 25. 31-46;   c. Eph. 4. 32.

15. Which verses in Psalm 103 refer to God as one who forgives?

Opinion and Research

16. When one person forgives another, what are the most important results for them? Give reasons for your answer.

17. People often say that they do not believe that God could forgive them. The author gives one reason why people say this.
    a. Do you think many people refuse forgiveness for the reason the author gives?
    b. What other reasons could there be?

18. There was a boy who twice stole valuable things from his father and sold them and spent the money. Each time his father forgave him and received him back. But a friend said, "You are encouraging your son to steal by treating him like this." What do you think?

19. It has been said that no race has proverbs or folk-stories which show the need to forgive, and that the Christian Gospel alone shows this. Can you discover any traditional sayings in your own language, or any other language, which contradict this statement?

Jesus' Parables and our own Parables, Fables, etc.

I TEACHING BY PARABLES

This was Jesus' chief way of teaching. He did not lecture nor teach His disciples creeds to learn. He told them stories, and proverbs which were like little stories.

We have seen in this book that these stories and proverbs were about things that were well-known to the listeners (seeds, money, journeys, etc.). They described things which the listeners could see in their minds as He spoke.

We have also seen that, by this method, Jesus did more than teach people to *think*. He also aroused their *feelings* and led them to take *decisions*. Such teaching was for the whole of a person, not for his mind alone.

But if Jesus has given us such an example of how to teach, we have to consider our own methods. It seems that we should not only learn from His parables and tell them to others; we should also use His methods.

This leads to questions such as these: "What is the difference between His parables and those which we invent today?" "Can our fables and our dreams be used as parables?" In the next few pages we attempt to answer such questions.

II JESUS' PARABLES

If we are to compare His parables with our own parables and fables, it will be useful first to recollect some points which have already been made about His parables:

1. They were about ordinary and well-known things, in order to show what our ordinary lives can become.

2. They were about ordinary things of this world because Jesus believed that God's world is one. The same God gives life and power to seeds in the ground and to men and women in their lives. This is the reason why a story about a farmer sowing seeds can give truth about our lives today.

3. Some of them were probably stories of events that actually took place while Jesus was teaching. Perhaps the "Good Samaritan" was someone who took care of a wounded Jew during the life-time of Jesus.

4. They were chosen by Jesus Himself. This is why they are specially important to us.

5. They tell us about Jesus Himself. For example, in the parable of a Woman and her Money, Jesus did not just say that God looks for "lost" people. He said:

a. God looks for the "lost" and this is the new teaching which I bring you.

b. It is my own work to look for the "lost" ones.

c. As you listen to my story God offers you a share in caring for such people.

6. They cannot be understood unless we remember also what Jesus taught at other times. We might, for example, read the parable of a Widow and a Magistrate and think that God was unjust. But from the rest of Jesus' teaching we know that He is not.

III OUR OWN PARABLES

What "parables" can Christians make today? How should they be compared to Jesus' parables? We shall try to answer such questions by studying some kinds of "parables" which we make and use today.

1. *Our own stories and circumstances*

Jesus made stories from the things that were known to His listeners, and we are right to do the same. And we do it by keeping our eyes open to see that God is at work in the world around us. All Jesus' parables are about God being at work and about people making their answer to what God does.

Perhaps we are teaching that people need to be renewed by God in their lives, and as we are speaking we see that it is raining. So we can use the rain which renews the ground as the subject for our parable.

Sometimes famous men make parables which are remembered for a long time. Many readers will know the parable of the piano which Kweggir Aggrey of Ghana told. He was teaching that all races must work together, and said, "You can play a tune of sorts on the white keys, and you can play a tune of sorts on the black keys; but for harmony you must use both the black and the white."

Our own stories are important for two reasons. First because some of the things that Jesus talked about in His parables are no longer well-known to people today. Many people who now use electric light do not know what an oil-lamp is like (Luke 15. 8). Secondly, because some things that Jesus talked about were well-known to His hearers but not to everyone alive at that time. He spoke about keeping sheep because His hearers kept sheep. If He had been speaking in the North of Canada (where sheep cannot live) He would not have talked about the Shepherd and his Sheep.

So today the truth has to be expressed through things that are known to the hearers. For example, a speaker was telling a congregation how to start afresh after they had done wrong. He said, "Admit it to God. Ask Him to forgive you and to help you to make a fresh start." Then he said, "A rusty bicycle gets more rusty if you leave it. If you want to use it again, you must scrape off the rust and paint it. If you don't, it falls to pieces."

Another speaker was saying that all men need to receive God's Spirit. He said, "The car in which I came today stopped on the hill because it ran out of petrol." That was his parable.

Our stories can be about things that happen all the time, like rain falling and bicycles getting rusty. Or they can be about a special event in the life of someone. A speaker was talking about loving our neighbour. First he told the parable of the Travellers on the Road. Then he said, "Some years ago, when there was violent anti-government action in South Africa, two men blew up a factory. One of them, Vuyisile Mini, was found guilty and condemned to death. Later he was offered a life sentence if he would give the police the name of the friend with whom he had worked. He refused to betray his friend, and was executed." The speaker was not praising Vuyisile's violence. He was telling a parable to show the power of God in the faithfulness of Vuyisile to his friend.

Nothing can take the place of Jesus' parables, because it was He who told them. But we are right to follow His example and to make our own.

2. *Myths*

Every nation has its own old stories or "myths". They are traditional stories about great men of the past and often contain truth about mankind. A well-known one is the "myth" of Isis and Osiris of Egypt. Osiris was a good king, who was killed by his brother Set, but made alive again by his sister Isis. (This story is connected with the River Nile which seems to "die" every year when there is only a little water in it, and seems to "rise again" when the rains come.)

This is different from Jesus' parables because it is not about ordinary events, and because the people who first told it did not share Jesus' knowledge of God. Yet it can be used by Christians because:

a. There is truth in it, and all truth is God's truth. It is true that new life comes through dying. See John 12. 24: "Unless a grain of wheat falls into the earth and dies, it remains alone; but if it dies, it bears much fruit."

b. It prepared for what Jesus did. The rising of King Osiris was only a story, but it prepared people's minds for when Jesus actually did rise.

But not all folk-stories and myths can be used in this way. Some myths carry with them a message that is not true, e.g. that man can only live through cruelty. The story of the girl Hainumele, told in a part of the South Pacific, seems to be of this sort. A man called Ameta cut his finger and the blood fell on to a flower. Where the blood had fallen Hainumele was born. As she grew up she became a dancer. While dancing at a festival she was killed by the other dancers. Ameta then cut up her body and buried the pieces in the ground. Wherever a piece had been buried vegetables grew. So Ameta and the others had food to eat.

Some stories seem to be saying that man can only live by deceit. Other myths carry a message that everything happens by chance and that there is no good power in control of the world.

We have to judge between those myths that can be used to teach what is true and those that cannot.

3. *Fables*

The same is true about fables, stories told about animals. The fable of the Lion and the Rat may be taken as an example. Lion and Rat met on a path in the forest. Rat said, "Lion, I am only a rat, but please don't step on me." And Lion kindly put his foot somewhere else. Another time Lion was hunting deer and fell into a trap covered by a net. All the animals came and looked and said, "We are very sorry for you." Then Rat came and cut away the net with his teeth and set Lion free.

This is not a "parable" because animals do not show sympathy for a large animal who is in trouble. The author of this story has made them behave like human beings: he has not let them be real animals.

There is a second way in which such a story is not like Jesus' parables: it does not carry with it teaching which is specially Christian. The author seems to be saying, "If you are kind to other people they will be kind to you." There is some truth in this, but it is not the special teaching which Jesus came to give. And when we think of the way in which people treated Jesus, there does not seem to be much truth in it.

Yet a fable can be used. The rat in the story mentioned above can be made an example of people who are despised by the world but who are used by God. "He has exalted those of low degree" (Luke 1. 52). Or the net can illustrate the sinfulness from which Jesus came to set us free. In such cases the teaching is contained in a simple story (like a parable) and it will be remembered for that reason.

4. *Proverbs*

Our national proverbs, although they are very short, are like our fables and myths. They have been handed down to us from the time when people were not Christian. Therefore they cannot of themselves point to the special teaching which Jesus came to give. In spite of this they can be used.

a. They tell us truly what men and women are like and what are some of their needs. The proverb: "All that glitters is not gold" tells us something about man's temptation to pretend to be what he is not. We need not be surprised that truth is given to us by these means, because all the world is God's. But there is something *more* that God wants to show us, for which this proverb can prepare us. The "something more" is what Jesus showed in such teaching as "There is nothing hidden that will not be known" (Matt. 10. 26).

b. They can point to special Christian teaching although they do not contain it. The proverb, "The stick in your neighbour's house does not drive away the leopard in your own doorway", can be well used to support the Christian teaching that a man must make his own decision whether he will follow Christ. "What do *you* think of the Christ?" (Matt. 22. 42.)

5. *Dreams*

Our dreams are different from the parables of Christ in many ways:

a. Events often occur in dreams which are unlike ordinary life. We fly through the air, or the man to whom we are talking turns into an eagle.

b. Very many dreams are confused, and very many are therefore impossible to interpret.

c. In the case of Jesus' parables we can be guided by the way in which others have interpreted them over many years; in the case of our dreams this is of course impossible.

d. We know that it is easy to make the mistake of interpreting Jesus' parables in a way that pleases us rather than in the way that He Himself intended. (We remember those who used the parable of a Host and His Guests to teach that it was right to force others to become Christians— p. 65.) But in dreams it is even more likely that the dreamer will give an interpretation that pleases him rather than try to find the true interpretation.

But in spite of this there are some dreams which can be compared to a parable, that is to say:

They point to the needs of the one who dreams;

They do this in the form of a story or part of a story;

The message is hidden and only someone who is ready can receive it.

Here is one of the dreams of which the Bible tells us. St Peter dreamt that out of the sky came a ship's sail, on which were animals. Some of these were animals which Jews were forbidden to eat. Three times a voice told St Peter to eat them because God had made them. Each time he said that he could not because they were unclean. Then the sail went back into the sky (see Acts 10. 9-16).

Through this dream St Peter found out something about himself and about his own needs. He discovered thoughts which had been in him before the dream but which he had not known. He was a Jewish Christian and up to that time had never eaten food with Christians who were not Jews. For a long time he had been thinking that perhaps he ought to eat with such Christians, but it was through this dream that these thoughts became clear to him. Then he had the courage to take action; he sat down to eat with Cornelius, the Roman, the non-Jew.

We can say, therefore, that sometimes a person has a dream through which he sees the truth about himself more clearly. It may be truth from which he usually hides because he does not like it. A woman who had been quarrelling with her married daughter had a dream that she was watching a mother bird. This bird first fed her young and then ate them up. The woman was angry with the mother bird and woke up feeling unhappy. When she thought about the dream, she said to herself, "Perhaps that bird is what I am. Perhaps that is how I treat my daughter, not letting her live her own life."

From this we can see something else about a dream: that through it we can see what are the things in which we especially need God's help. The woman saw that she needed His help in the way in which she treated her daughter.

Through a dream we can sometimes also discover what decisions we should take. The head of a small Maternity Clinic had been invited to a meeting in the senior Maternity Hospital 200 miles away. She told the nurses in the clinic that "she was not sure if she had time to go". That night she had a dream that she was the pilot of an aeroplane. She got into the plane and started the engine, but she was too frightened to leave the ground. Instead she sat talking and laughing with the mechanics. That was her dream. (Some people might have interpreted it as a warning that an accident would take place if the journey was made. But that would have been a mistake, because it is ourselves and our feelings that we learn about through dreams.) When the woman thought about it, she saw that it had been about her own fears; she saw that she was afraid that if she went to the meeting the methods she used in her clinic would be criticized. The choice she had to make had become clear: either to go and risk criticism, or to stay and avoid it.

We can say, therefore, that some dreams can be like a parable. And we can thank God for giving us minds which produce such dreams. But we have to take care. When we say that dreams can be like parables, we must interpret them as carefully as we interpret Jesus' parables. How can we tell if the message which we believe we have received through a dream is a true message? This is a hard question. But we shall be on the right lines if we place this "message" alongside the deepest truths which we know about God and man. If this message contradicts such truths then we should not call it a true message.

NOTE: The word "dream" is used here as something that we experience in sleep. It is not used to mean "day-dreams", i.e. idle thoughts about things we should like to happen in the future.

A LIFE IS A PARABLE

Jesus' parables cannot be separated from the rest of His life. All that He did was a parable because it showed people that the power of God was at work in man: God's power at work in Him.

This is true of certain things which He did because He wanted to teach a lesson. He chose a donkey on which to ride into Jerusalem in order to show that He was a King who would rule in peace, not by force (Mark 11. 2). It is also true of His miracles. When He cured a blind man, He was showing that He was the Messiah who had come to help people to see in their hearts and to see with their eyes.

All His life was a parable. This is partly the reason why St John's Gospel says that Jesus was "the Word" (John 1. 14).

This concerns ourselves. We are right to tell Jesus' parables, and to make our own. But we also *are* parables. It is possible for us to be good parables, through which people may see that God is at work in man, and through which they may make their own decision concerning Him.

STUDY SUGGESTIONS FOR SPECIAL NOTE C

Word Study

1. Which of the following descriptions is correct for (*a*) a parable? (*b*) a myth? (*c*) a fable? (*d*) a proverb?
   A story about animals.
   A story about ordinary things to show what our ordinary lives can become.
   A short saying often containing truth about mankind.
   A traditional folk-story often containing truth about mankind.

2. The word "story" as used in English today can have several different meanings. One meaning is "a true account of what happened". What two other meanings can you think of?

Review of Content

3. What was Jesus' chief way of teaching?

4. Why did Jesus talk about ordinary things in His parables?

5. Why do we call the story of the Lion and the Rat a "fable" rather than a "parable"?

E

6. In what ways are dreams different from parables?

7. *a.* What did St Peter find out about himself through his dream of the ship's sail?
   b. What did the woman find out about herself who dreamt she was the pilot of an aeroplane?

8. What is meant by saying that "people are parables"?

Bible Study

9. This chapter contains three parables which might be told today:
   i. The Rusty Bicycle.
   ii. The Empty Petrol Tank.
   iii. The Faithful Friend.
   Which of these parables would you choose to illustrate a sermon with the text:
   a. Romans 8. 11;   *b.* John 15. 13;   *c.* Psalm 51. 10.

10. Many of Jesus' actions were also parables. For each of the following passages say (*a*) what the action was, (*b*) in what way it was a parable.
    Mark 2. 15;   Mark 10. 46-52.

Opinion and Research

11. "Jesus made stories from the things that were known to His listeners, and we are right to do the same."
    a. Write a parable based on Luke 18. 10-14, not using the words "Pharisees" or "tax-collectors", but using words and names which are well-known to most people living today.
    b. Write a parable based on Luke 15. 4-7, not using the word "sheep", but using language suitable for townspeople who have never seen sheep.
    c. Write a parable based on Matt. 13. 47, 48, not using the words "fish" or "sea", but using language suitable for people who live far from rivers or seas.

12. *a.* What makes a "folk-story" or "myth" suitable for use by a Christian preacher?
    b. Give an example of a suitable folk-story and explain how a Christian teacher could use it.

13. A West African proverb says, "Being friendly with a water-seller does not take away your dirt."
    a. Could you use this in a sermon?
    b. If so, how? If not, why not?

14. The author writes of dreams as pointing to the needs of the one who dreams.
    a. Tell a dream you or a friend of yours has had.
    b. What did it show concerning the needs of the dreamer?

Chapter 11. Bridesmaids and a Bridegroom

Matt. 25. 1-13
The Parable of the Ten Virgins

I OUTLINE

This is a story about a wedding, in which the bridegroom and his friends went to fetch the bride from her home.

The bride had ten bridesmaids, and they set out from her house to welcome the bridegroom and his friends. It was evening and they all took little lamps with them containing oil. Five of them took some extra oil.

They waited on the side of the road for a long time and in the end they all fell asleep in the warm night air. At about midnight one of them saw the lights of the bridegroom and his friends in the distance. She woke up the others and they all began to get their lamps ready. They had to rub off the burnt part of the wick and put fresh oil in and light them again.

But the five girls who had not brought extra oil with them could not refill their lamps. They said to the others, "Lend us some oil. Ours is finished. It would be against our custom for us to welcome the bride-groom without lamps." But the others said that they could not do this. They said, "There is still a long time to go before we reach the bride's house. If we give you some of our oil, our lamps and your lamps might all go out before we get there. You try to buy some. Some oil-sellers may still be awake." So the five who had not brought extra went off to buy oil.

While they were away, the bridegroom came, and the five girls whose lamps were alight went with him and his friends to the bride's house. Later the other five arrived at the house, and found the door shut. They knocked loudly on it. It was opened by the bridegroom himself. But he did not know who they were, and told them to go away and not to disturb the party.

II SEEING THE ORIGINAL SITUATION

The situation
If we want to find out when Jesus first told this parable and why He told it, we must look at the parable itself. We see then that it is chiefly about people who were ready and people who were not. We ask "To whom was Jesus giving a warning? Whom was He telling to be ready?"

In the Gospels we read of two special groups of people to whom Jesus often gave just this kind of warning:

103

1. The religious leaders. To them Jesus was saying, "You and your nation have not done what God chose you to do. You are bringing punishment upon yourselves. The time of disaster is getting nearer. It is not too late for you to change your ways." See Matt. 23, e.g., "Alas for you, lawyers and Pharisees, hypocrites! . . . . You snakes . . . . how can you escape being condemned to hell?" (vv. 29, 33, NEB). (We know now that they did not listen to Jesus. The city of Jerusalem was destroyed by the Romans in AD 70 and the Jewish nation scattered.

2. His disciples. To them Jesus said, "I have come into the world to announce that God is ruling over men in a new way. Men either decide for me, or they decide against me. As they decide, so they are judged. There are many times when these decisions have to be made. The greatest of these times will be the time of my death. Be ready!" "He began to teach them that the Son of Man had to undergo great sufferings . . . . to be put to death . . . . 'Anyone who wishes to be a follower of mine must leave self behind' " (Mark 8. 31, 34, NEB). (We know that they were not ready. When He was arrested, they "all ran away". Matt. 26. 56, NEB.)

The chief message of this parable, therefore, is this:

"Be ready. Be ready for each situation in which you will be judged by God. Wise people get ready for things that are coming."

By saying this, Jesus was urging His listeners to get ready for *all* events. They must be ready for those events which were near at hand (such as His own death), those events which were further away (such as the destruction of Jerusalem), and that event which we call "the Last Judgement" or His "Coming Again".

Suggested Application

1. Times of testing or judgement.

In the parable the coming of the bridegroom was the time when the girls were judged or tested (whether they were ready or not).

The Greek work for judgement is "crisis", and this is a word which is often used now for any dangerous situation in the life of a person or of a nation. Newspapers often talk about a "food crisis" when they mean that there is a shortage of food. But they also mean that in this situation people judge the government. Have the government prepared for this, or not? Have they got ready extra supplies of food?

In our lives there are many times of "crisis", and in each one we are being tested and asked, "Did you prepare for *this*?" Some of these times of testing seem very unimportant at the time, others are more easily seen to be important. Here are some of these times of testing:

A school or college examination;
An illness;

104

A temptation to do wrong;
Being given some new responsibility;
Having a quarrel with a friend;
Marriage;
Being opposed by fellow-workers;
Failure to have children in marriage;
Being opposed by our own children who are growing up;
The death of a husband or wife;
Our own death.
To this list we must add:
The Last Judgement of mankind.

In each of these times of testing, we show what kind of people we are, and each nation shows what kind of nation it is. All these times (and very many others like them) make us what we become. So each one is important. It is a serious mistake to say, "The important thing is the way I live just before I die."

2. Getting ready.

What makes someone ready for these times of testing?

Very many things join in making someone ready. For example:

a. The many *decisions* he takes. The way he does this gives him his "character"; it makes him the sort of person he is. Then when he is suddenly given responsibility or suddenly has suffering to bear, his character is strong enough to stand the test.

b. What he really *believes* makes a difference to the decisions he takes and to his character.

c. At the same time it is his "*character*" that leads him to accept those beliefs and also to take his decisions.

We can see all this happening in a friend if we watch him growing up as God intends and becoming "ready" in all these different ways. People saw Yona Kanamuzeyi of Rwanda growing in this way. When he was captured by enemy soldiers and told that he was going to die, he said, "You kill me because I am a Christian. Well, I am ready to die as a Christian."

When Mary of Orange. who became Queen of England in 1687, was told that she was just about to die, her chaplain asked, "Shall I come and say prayers with you?" She said, "My friend, I did not leave this matter till this hour."

The same is true of a nation. The people of a nation cannot face a great crisis such as hunger or war unless they are ready. Several countries at this time face a serious shortage of nurses in their hospitals and their governments call for people who have "vocation" to take up nursing. But no country gets nurses with vocation unless throughout the years children and adults have been led to believe in God who "calls" people to such work and gives them skill to do it. In Communist

105

countries there are many people with vocation, but it is "the State" not God which "calls".

3. No one else can make us ready for great times of testing. We must become ready ourselves. In the parable the girls who had oil could not lend it to the others: "Buy some for yourselves", or, in present-day words, "*My* battery would not fit *your* torch." It is our daily decisions which prepare us: e.g. to pray or not to pray, to tell the truth or not to tell the truth, to be courageous or to be cowardly.

4. Getting ready occupies the whole of our lives. No one can prepare once and for all by being baptized or by offering his life to God on one single day.

III SEEING OUR OWN SITUATION

Let us go back to the story and to the time when the girls made a choice as they left the bride's house and went out to meet the bridegroom. Their choice was: Should they take extra oil, or not?

This is our situation, over and over again. God puts in front of us a moment when we make a choice. Each time we either get more ready for the great times of testing, or we fail to get ready.

Readers will easily think of examples of this. Here are three examples, three people speaking of times when they are tested:

1. I am a parent and my small child is behaving badly. What am I to do? Do I think chiefly of the trouble she is causing me and so lose my temper? Or do I think chiefly of her needs and control my temper in order to help her? If I learn to choose the second of these, I am preparing for times when this girl is growing up. Then she may find that life is full of difficulties and need my help and sympathy. Will she be able to rely on me then? Will I be ready?

2. I have applied for many jobs and been unsuccessful. Do I despair and believe that God is against me? Or can I believe that He loves me and will lead me to a job? If I learn to choose the second of these I am growing in faith and being made ready for greater tests. I become ready for the time when perhaps I meet opposition from my fellow-workers and must stand on my own. I become ready for the time when perhaps an illness tests my faith and courage.

3. I am a girl cooking a meal. I spill the soup which the whole family was going to have. I can easily find a younger child whom I can blame. Or I can accept it as my fault and apologize. If I can do the second of these, I am being made ready for greater tests, e.g. for times of difficulty in married life when an honest apology can restore love; for the time when I shall give an account of my whole life to God and when He offers peace to one who can make an honest confession, "Lord, have mercy on me, a sinner."

"Be ready for each situation in which you will be judged . . . Getting ready occupies the whole of our lives."

How many hours did these athletes spend in training for this "time of crisis"?

NOTE: It is important to notice that in this parable Jesus was not simply saying, "A man reaps what he sows." That is a true saying and comes from Galatians 6. 7 (NEB). But Jesus was saying more than that:

a. As in all His parables Jesus was saying, "I offer you the best life, and you *can* have it. Don't be so foolish as to miss it! Everyone makes preparations for something. I beg you to make preparations for the best things, for the fullest life, for 'eternal life' in which you can be held firm by God Himself."

b. He also taught that a man is given *more* than he has sown, i.e. that God treats us better than we deserve (see Chapter 4). This does not contradict His warning that we must be ready; it is to be remembered alongside that warning.

NOTES

a. Other Parables. There are other parables in which also the chief message seems to be, "Be ready for each great time of testing". Luke 12 contains three of them:

The Waiting Servants (vv. 35-38).

A Thief at Night (vv. 39, 40).

A Servant Left in Charge (vv. 42-46).

For other parables of this kind, see pp. 118 and 119, Note **a.**

b. The kingdom of heaven shall be compared to ten maidens (v. 1). This verse does not mean that the Kingdom of Heaven is like ten girls. A better way to translate the words is, "The Kingdom of Heaven is like this. There was once a wedding at which ten girls took lamps . . . ." See note **c** on p. 85.

We remember that the "Kingdom of Heaven" means "the loving God ruling as supreme authority, working in the world with love and power". It is not a *place.* (See note c, p. 48)

c. The bridegroom was delayed (v. 5). As we read this story, the important part of it is the phrase "the wise took flasks of oil", that is to say, their readiness.

But we should note that some writers have interpreted it rather differently. They have said that the story is an allegory, i.e. a story in which each part was intended to have a different lesson. They say: "The bridegroom is Jesus the Messiah. The delay of the bridegroom is the delay between the telling of the parable by Jesus and His Second Coming. The chief teaching is, 'Be faithful and keep awake, during your long wait for the Second Coming.' Verse 13 is the important verse in this parable."

Some reasons why this interpretation does not seem to be the right one are:

1. The story does not seem to be about keeping awake or sleeping. All of them went to sleep. It is a story about being ready.
2. Jesus' custom was usually to tell parables, i.e. stories with one chief message, rather than allegories. Allegories are more used by teachers who write down their teaching: Jesus' way was to tell His stories as part of a conversation.
3. In His teaching Jesus used to urge people to face their present problems. That is why we believe that in this parable Jesus was saying: "Be ready for each testing time," "Be ready for my death which is now approaching." It is hard to believe that He was chiefly telling them to be ready for His Second Coming since this was a very long way off indeed.
4. But His Second Coming is included in the "times of testing" for which we must get ready.
See Special Note B, p. 67.

d. Went in with him to the marriage feast (v. 10). This feast seems to have been at the bride's house (as suggested in the Outline above). If so, then the wedding itself took place later at the bridegroom's house. But we cannot be sure because the story in Matt. 25 is not (and does not need to be) complete.

e. The door was shut (v. 10) . . **I do not know you** (v. 12). It sounds as if the bridegroom was cruel to keep them out, and it is easy to interpret the words wrongly. We should note that:
1. This is a parable and not an allegory. So we do not say that "the bridegroom is Jesus" and "the door is heaven".
2. Nevertheless it is true that those who get ready are divided from those who do not. Although God wants everyone to find eternal life (1 Tim. 2. 4), it is possible for us to refuse this gift. We can refuse it by our actions and by the choices we make.

STUDY SUGGESTIONS FOR CHAPTER 11

Word Study

1. The words "character" and "vocation" are used in this chapter. Give examples from everyday life to show the meaning of each.
2. *a.* Which *three* of the following four words have the same meaning as "a time of crisis" as used in this chapter? See p. 104.
   testing   disaster   turning-point   judgement-day
   b. Read the headlines of the newspapers of the last two or three weeks and see if they contain the word "crisis".
   i. If they do, is the word used in the same way as it is used in this chapter?
   ii. If it is not, how is it used?

Review of Content

3. What were the two special groups of people to whom Jesus probably told the parable of Bridesmaids and a Bridegroom?

4. At what time of the day did the wedding take place?

5. In which part of the story do we read about some girls making preparations and five failing to do so?

6. Why did the girls with extra oil not lend some to the others?

7. Which two of the following people or groups of people were ready for their "time of testing"?
   Jesus' disciples
   Yona Kanamuzeyi
   The bridesmaids who brought extra oil
   Jewish lawyers in the time of Jesus

8. Who divides those who are ready from those who are not?

9. Are the following true or untrue? Give reasons for your answer in each case.
   a. All the ten girls took oil in their lamps.
   b. Five of them kept awake and five went to sleep.
   c. When Jesus died, His disciples were not ready.
   d. Matt. 25. 10 shows that God shuts the door of heaven against those who are not ready.

Bible Study

10. *a.* Write out very briefly in your own words the three stories in Luke 12:
      i. vv. 35-38; ii. vv. 39, 40; iii. vv. 42-46.
    b. In what way are these stories like the parable of Bridesmaids and a Bridegroom?

11. Read Isaiah 1. 15-20.
    a. What sort of behaviour was Isaiah attacking?
    b. What would result from this behaviour, according to Isaiah?
    c. In what way are these verses like this parable?

Opinion and Research

12. "Getting ready occupies the whole of our lives. No one can prepare once and for all by being baptized or by offering his life to God on a single day."
    a. What is your opinion?
    b. What guidance do the following give you?
      John 3. 3; 1 Thess. 4. 10 and 5. 6; 1 Tim. 4. 7.

13. "The people of a nation cannot face a crisis unless they are ready."
    Give an example of one occasion when the people of your country
    a. have shown that they were ready;
    b. have shown or are showing that they are not ready.

14. A girl reading this chapter said, "If I accepted this interpretation
    of the parable every little decision I took would become too
    important. I should become anxious and worried." Do you agree
    with her? Give reasons for your answer.

15. a. Give two traditional proverbs which have the same meaning as
       "A man reaps what he sows."
    b. In what way is the parable of Bridesmaids and a Bridegroom
       different from these proverbs?

16. Add three examples from everyday life to the list of "times of
    crisis" given in this chapter. See p. 105.

17. Jesus warned His hearers that disaster would follow unless they
    changed their ways.
    a. Do preachers in your Church speak in this way?
    b. Ought they to?
    c. Should they use the kind of strong language Jesus used in
       Matt. 23? Give reasons for your answers to b. and c.

18. a. When it becomes clear that an ill person is going to die soon,
       should he be told? Give reasons for your answer.
    b. If so, by whom should he be told?
    c. Would you yourself want to be told if you were soon to die?

Chapter 12. A Householder and his Servants

Matt. 25. 14-30
The Parable of the Talents

I OUTLINE

A rich man was going on a journey, and decided to protect his money from thieves by entrusting it to three of his servants. He told them to trade with it and to give an account of it when he returned.

One servant was given five bags of gold, and immediately started to trade with them. Another servant had two bags, and he also began trading. The third had been given only one bag. But he was afraid that he might lose it if he traded with it, so he wrapped it up in a cloth and buried it safely in the ground.

After some time the owner came back. He asked each of them how they had used his money. When he heard that the first two men had increased the money, he was very pleased with them, and promised to reward them.

Then he came to the third man. This man gave him back the bag of gold, and said, "Here is your money, sir. I have kept it safe for you. But I did not trade with it because you would have been very angry if I had lost it." Then the owner was indeed angry. He said, "I instructed you to trade with the money, and you have not done so. You have been a useless servant to me, and must leave my house." And he gave the bag of gold to the servant who had traded with five bags.

II SEEING THE ORIGINAL SITUATION

The situation

St Matthew has not answered the questions, "Why did Jesus tell this story?" or, "To whom did He tell it?" So we must try to answer these questions by studying the story itself. When we do this we see that the important part of the story is the last part, that is to say, the part about the man who failed to use what the rich man had entrusted to him.

So we ask, "What people during the time of Jesus' ministry were failing to use the gifts entrusted to them by God?" or, "Who was in danger of failing in this way?" There were two groups of people like this: the Jewish religious leaders and the disciples of Jesus. The parable could have been told to either of them.

1. It may have been told to the religious leaders of the Jewish people, especially some of the Pharisees.

They had experienced God's care in a special way. They had been given opportunities to live as His sons. As leaders they were expected to share their experience with other people. But:

a. Some of them were so afraid that they might be spoiled by meeting people whose religion was different, that they failed to share their experience with others.

b. They were so anxious to keep themselves pure that they would not listen to any new interpretations of the Old Testament (such as Jesus gave them).

c. They so much wanted to obey God's will themselves that they forgot to help other people to do so.

d. In their position as leaders they made a profit for themselves out of their knowledge of God's will. Their leadership became a burden upon poor people instead of a help to them (see Matt. 23, especially vv. 4, 6, 13).

In these ways they failed to accept their responsibility.

It is true that in many ways the scribes and Pharisees were good people. They were sincere and really wanted to obey God's laws. But, for the reasons we have noticed above, they were indeed like the man who failed to trade with the bag of gold entrusted to him. And so Jesus probably gave them this parable as a serious warning. His warning was:

"*You must give account to God for the way in which you have used the experience He has given you. So far you have not used it well. Change your ways before it is too late.*"

2. Perhaps the parable was also told to Jesus' disciples.

The disciples had been given the gift of Jesus Himself. But what were they doing with this Gift? Were they enjoying Him privately, like the servant burying the bag? Or were they ready to share their knowledge of Him with others so that the Church could increase?

When Jesus told this parable He knew that He would not be seen on earth much longer. So this matter was urgent. After His Ascension His work of spreading the Gospel would become the disciples' work. So, if Jesus told this parable to them, He was saying, "You will have to give account to God for the way in which you use the Gospel. Share it with all the world. Do not be afraid to do this. It is your responsibility: do not leave it to other people to do it." (We are reminded of Jesus' words to them: "You are salt to the world." Matt. 5. 13, NEB.)

The message of this parable, therefore, is like the message of the parable of Bridesmaids and a Bridegroom (see Chapter 11). There is the same warning, "Do this before it is too late."

113

"God expects Christians to use their gifts, their whole selves, with *courage*."
Pacific island fishermen earn a living by leaping into deep water — —

Suggested Application

1. God expects Christians to give *account* to Him of what they do with their lives and their "gifts".

Above all, we are called to give account of our whole selves, i.e. what sort of people we are. But we must also give account of our "gifts", e.g. our experience of God being at work in our lives, our money, our time, our being parents, our being citizens, the things that each of us is able to do well. (It is because of this parable that the English word for these things is "talents".)

God is not "hard" (v. 24) because He makes us give account of our lives. He does it because He is a Father and wants His sons to enjoy working together with Him. "Working together with Him, then, we entreat you not to accept the grace of God in vain" (2 Cor. 6. 1). And it is true that when we live our lives like this, they become fuller and greater lives. When St Paul's Cathedral was being built in London under the direction of the architect Wren, a visitor came to see the work. He asked some of the workmen what they were doing. One said, "I am cutting stone." Another said, "I am earning my wages." A third said, "I am helping Sir Christopher Wren to build a cathedral." All the answers were true, but the man who gave the third answer was living his life more fully than the others.

114

— — to spear their catch.

2. God expects Christians to *use* what He has given them.

It was not enough for the servant to keep the bag of gold safe: he was expected to trade with it. So it is not enough to keep our "gifts" safe. If they are not used and increased they are taken away.

Our bodily powers are taken away if they are not used. The Society for the Prevention of Cruelty to Children reported that a little girl was forced by her parents to pretend that she had only one leg. This was in order that she should go out and beg for them. So her left leg was tied up, out of sight. She was like this for so long that in the end she could not use her left leg at all. There was no power left in it.

The same is true of our power to speak another language. If we do not use it, we lose it and forget that language. The same is true about praying. If we do not pray, we forget how to pray.

It is true about the Church. Members of a Christian congregation may say, "See what a good congregation is here!" But unless new members are being brought in, that congregation is slowly dying away.

3. God expects Christians to use their gifts, their whole selves, with *courage*, and to take risks.

The servant in the parable was so frightened that he never tried to trade with the gold. Because of his fear he was untrustworthy. We have seen above that the Pharisees were afraid in the same way. In many parables Jesus praises people who take risks and are not afraid to do so:

The woman who kept on asking the magistrate to hear her case (Luke 18. 1-8);

The farmer who sowed his seed even on stony and thorny ground (Mark 4. 3-8);

The traveller who went to a wounded man at a time when the robbers might still be near (Luke 10. 29-37);

The shepherd who left ninety-nine sheep in order to go and look for the one that was lost (Luke 15. 3-7);

The father who gave his son money and made him free to leave home (Luke 15. 11-32);

The owner of the vineyard who sent his own son, knowing that he might be killed (Mark 12. 1-12).

Christians are right to take great care of the Church and the Gospel which are God's gifts. But some risks must be taken as we use them for the sake of others and as we allow them to increase. Here is one example of a Christian who understood this. He was an Indian student who had recently become a Christian. Many of his old friends were not Christians and were engaged in organizing a political party which used many dishonest practices. There were some Christians who begged this student to keep away from his old friends. They were afraid that he might lose his new faith. But he said that he must continue to treat them as his friends. He said, "Who will they listen to if I separate myself from them?" (More examples of this are considered in Part III of this chapter.)

4. To sum up, God expects Christians to be His *responsible* sons. Our religion has two sides, just as a coin has two sides. One is to depend on God as children depend on their parents, the other is to become trustworthy and responsible. It is the second of these to which Jesus points in this parable.

His Church cannot do His work in the world unless the members are both dependent and responsible. The servants in this parable all depended on their master for their work and wages; two of them were also responsible in the way in which they used the money. But we often fail in this. Sometimes we fail by being merely dependent: we obey God, lean on Him, submit to His authority, and ask for His strength, but fail to fight for Him against the world's evil. Sometimes we fail in the opposite way: we are willing to accept responsibility, and we work and fight for God in the world, but forget how greatly we depend upon God's grace. A mature Christian is one who depends upon God. He knows his own weakness, but at the same time he lives as a responsible grown-up son of His. We are God's sons and daughters, not His babies.

III SEEING OUR OWN SITUATION

We are the three servants in this parable. Throughout each day God entrusts to us His very precious things, and we use them responsibly and well, or we do not. And, each time, the power of God is at hand to help us to use them well and to use them with courage because they belong to Him. A few examples will show that this is indeed our own situation today.

1. A student wakes up in the morning and sees that there is half-an-hour before the first college activity. He knows that the half-hour belongs to God and has been lent to him. How shall he use it? Examinations are near and he has prepared for them well, but he can do some extra revision. He knows also that he can use the time for prayer. It needs courage to use the time for prayer because he knows that some other students will be doing extra revision. He takes the risk and says his prayers.

2. A minister finds that some of the words and music of the Church services to which the people are accustomed are no longer suitable. Newcomers to the Church and young people find them especially unsuitable. The leader of a Christian congregation must give account to God of the way in which he leads them, because they belong to Him. What shall he do? He can keep things as they are (and most of the older members of his congregation hope that he will do that). Or he can plan some new ways of worship in consultation with others. If he does this he will be taking a risk: he will probably make some mistakes; some of his plans may not be successful, and older members may be very troubled by changes. If he does not take this risk, what will happen to the younger members?

3. A boy is leaving school and must find work. His family has already arranged that he shall go into an office where his father knows the manager. He himself believes that God has given him a power by which he can help and care for sick and troubled people: he really wants to receive training as a teacher of deaf children. But it will need courage to do this: his family may say that he is being foolish and ungrateful; he may not be successful in his training course; he may not earn as much money as he would in the office and therefore have less with which to support his parents.

4. In a village congregation it has been the custom for the minister to make all the important decisions, e.g. how many services to hold, when to hold them, how to collect money, whom to visit, what to preach about, etc. A new minister has come and asks the congregation to share with him in making these decisions. At first they are afraid. "You are our father and our pastor," they say, "It is your work." Yet they and he are together responsible.

5. The leaders of one Church have been asked to consider union with another Church. What kind of agreement is right? On the one hand, they will not be faithful to God if they give up the truth which has been handed down to their Church through many generations. On the other hand they will not be faithful to God if they do nothing to join with other Christians because of their fears (e.g. fears as to what might happen after union has taken place). This was the situation in South India before the Union took place there in 1947. At one meeting a speaker said, "The demand to know where we are going — i.e. what might happen after Union — is one which no Christian has a right to make."

6. A Christian meets a foreigner who seems unhappy. Shall he keep silent, or shall he say a word of friendliness? If he speaks, there is a risk that the man may take offence or dislike being spoken to by a stranger.

In all these situations, God does not say, "You ought to act with more courage." He says, "I am with you and I will lead you as you 'trade with your gift'. You can rely on Me as you act as my responsible sons. By your action you show your faithfulness to Me."

NOTES

a. Other "Parables of Readiness". As we have seen, Jesus told many parables in order to prepare His hearers for things to come. He wanted to warn them and to encourage them. It is not possible to say today what was in the mind of Jesus when He first told each parable: but as far as we can see the parables of this kind are these:

Bridesmaids and a Bridegroom (Matt. 25. 1-13. See Chapter 11).

The Waiting Servants; a Thief at Night; a Servant Left in Charge (Luke 12. 35-46. See p. 108, Note a).

The Pounds (Luke 19. 11-27. See Note b below).

A Tree and its Fruit (Luke 6. 43-45); A Fig-Tree without Figs (Luke 13. 6-9). "While you have time, let the truth which you have received be used for the benefit of others!"

The Wicked Vine-Dressers (Mark 12. 1-11; Matt. 21. 33-43; Luke 20. 9-18). "I am giving you an opportunity to change your ways of living before it is too late."

Men going to the Magistrate (Matt. 5. 23-26; Luke 12. 54-59. See p. 31, numbered paragraph 1).

Finally, five parables in which the chief message was: "Make use of your opportunities of finding God and serving Him while they exist":

Two Builders (Matt. 7. 24-27; Luke 6. 47-49).

A Rich Fool (Luke 12. 16-20).

A Clever Agent (Luke 16. 1-8).

"God expects Christians to be his *responsible* sons and daughters."
    This woman exercises her responsibility as a citizen of Ghana by going to cast her vote in an election.

119

The Rich Man and Lazarus (Luke 16. 19-31).
The Wedding Clothes (Matt. 22. 11-14).

b. The Parable of the Pounds (Luke 19. 11-27). In St Luke's Gospel there is a parable which is very much like this one, and which seems to have the same central message. But it is different in these ways:

1. It seems to have become joined to another parable about a prince who goes away to be made king.

2. There are ten servants (instead of three) and they all receive the same amount.

3. The amount they receive is much smaller than in St Matthew's parable.

Either Jesus told this parable more than once, and did not always tell it in the same way; *or* St Matthew has given us Jesus' parable, and St Luke gives us a less accurate account of what Jesus said.

c. Talents (v. 15). A talent was a weight, not a coin; a talent of silver might buy more than £1,000 worth of goods today. But in this parable the word only means "a large amount of money". The NEB translation "five bags of gold", "three bags of gold", etc. is good.

d. He who had received the one talent (v. 18). This man was given one talent, the others had been given five and three talents. We are not all given equal gifts by God. (This was true of the disciples. Jesus chose out Peter and James and John to go with Him because they understood better than the others what He wanted.)

There is a temptation here. We may say, "If I had Mr X's powers, I could be a better Christian." But that is not so. We are simply told to "trade" with what we have and what we are. A good Christian, therefore, is someone who accepts himself and the gifts that God has given him; he uses in God's service whatever powers he has or whatever knowledge of God he has been given.

e. After a long time the master of those servants came (v. 19). Some Christians have regarded this verse as the central verse of the parable. They have said, "Jesus is here teaching about His own Second Coming. In the parable, Jesus is the 'master'."

It is possible that this is so, but it is not very likely. It is more probable that Jesus was telling His enemies and His disciples to be ready for something that would happen very soon indeed. See Note **c.** in chapter 11, pp. 108 and 109.

f. To every one who has will more be given (v. 29). From experience, we know that this is true. The more books that a student reads, the more likely he is to be able to read with speed and understanding. The person who has the deepest understanding of Jesus' teaching is the person who receives the most from reading the Gospels.

Jesus did not mean that God wants rich men to become richer. We know this from the rest of His teaching about money and rich people, e.g. Luke 1. 53; Mark 10. 23.

But some people believe that Jesus spoke vv. 29 and 30 at other times, and not as part of this parable. We find v. 29, separated from this parable, in Mark 4. 25, Matt. 13. 12, and Luke 8. 18; and we find something like v. 30 in Matt. 8. 12; 13. 42; 13. 50; and 22. 13.

STUDY SUGGESTIONS FOR CHAPTER 12

Word Study

1. *a.* The words "responsibility" and "dependence" are used in this chapter. Give examples from everyday life to show the meaning of each.
    b. Which *three* of the following words as used in the chapter are most closely connected with responsibility, and which *three* are most closely connected with dependence?
    courage   lean   reliable   baby   trustworthy   weakness

2. *a.* What was a "talent" at the time when Jesus spoke?
    b. What does the word mean in English now?

Review of Content

3. In what way did the servants in the parable studied in this chapter depend on their master?

4. What did the rich man tell his servants to do with his money while he was away on a journey?

5. What did the third servant do with his money?

6. Did Jesus tell the parable of a Householder and his Servants in order to warn His hearers or to condemn them?

7. In what way is this parable like the parable of Bridesmaids and a Bridegroom?

8. Remembering the examples given in this chapter, say what decision each of the following people had to take.
    a. The student who woke early.
    b. The boy who was leaving school.
    c. The village congregation.

9. *a.* What special teaching did Jesus want His hearers to learn through the parable of the Wicked Vine-dressers (Mark 12. 11)?
    b. Which verse expresses this teaching most clearly?

10. "Jesus did not mean (Matt. 25. 29) that God wants rich men to become richer."
    Give a verse from the New Testament about riches which shows that this is true.

121

Bible Study

11. Read the following parables recorded by St Luke and say in each case which verse best expresses the teaching: "While you have time find God and serve Him."
    a. 12. 16-20; *b.* 16. 1-8; *c.* 16. 19-31.

12. In what way is the teaching in each of the following verses like the teaching of this parable?
    a. Matt. 5. 13; *b.* 2 Cor. 6. 1; *c.* Phil. 2. 12.

13. Explain why we say that each of the following people "took risks".
    a. The Samaritan mentioned in Luke 10. 29-37.
    b. The father mentioned in Luke 15. 11-32.
    c. The woman mentioned in Luke 18. 1-8.

Opinion and Research

14. *a.* Why did the third man not trade with his money?
    b. Have you ever made the mistake of not taking part in a conversation or in some other useful activity? For what reasons did you not want to take part?
    c. Why do some people have the habit of accepting responsibility?

15. "If we do not use it, we lose it."
    Give an example from everyday life to show that this is true.

16. Do the members of the congregation which you know best accept responsibility for the Church, or do they leave the responsibility to the minister?

17. "A mature Christian is one who depends on God .... at the same time he lives as a responsible grown-up son of His."
    How might someone behave who:
    a. depends on God but not in a responsible way?
    b. accepts responsibility but does not want to depend on God?
    c. depends on God in a responsible way?

18. Choose three or four hymns which you often sing and say in each case whether they chiefly encourage dependence or chiefly encourage responsibility.

19. *a.* In what way did the rich man in the parable we have studied encourage his servants to become responsible?
    b. How can a parent or teacher encourage his children to be responsible?
    c. What things do unwise parents or teachers do which discourage their children from being responsible?

Key to Study Suggestions

PART I A WAY OF STUDYING THE PARABLES

1. *a. Situation:*   circumstances   happenings   events
   b. Application: message   lesson   interpretation
   See p. 2, line 16 onward, and p. 3, line 2 onward for the words as used in this chapter.
3. See p. 1, last 2 lines, and p. 2, lines 1-5.
4. See p. 2, last 2 lines, and p. 3, line 1.
5. *a.* See p. 4, lines 10-24.   6. See p. 1, last 4 lines.
   b. See p. 4, lines 7-24.   7. See p. 2, lines 35-38.
8. *a.* Untrue. See p. 2, lines 23 and 24.
   b. True. See p. 3, paragraph 2 *a.*.
   c. Untrue. See p. 3, paragraph 2 *c.*.
9. In Romans 5. 8 we read that God, because of His love, is concerned to rescue sinners.
10. John 1. 14 and Hebrew 4. 15.
13. For the stories about changes that are needed, see p. 4, lines 27-32, and p. 5, lines 2-6.
14. P. 4, line 19.

PART II CHAPTER 1. A TAILOR AND AN OLD COAT

1. *a. Grace:*   A kind of generosity   given in spite of sin
   b. Covenant: A kind of agreement   a reminder that we belong to God
3. *a.* The Parable of the Wine skins   4. See p. 7, last 12 lines.
   b. The same.   5. See p. 8, lines 8-10.
6. See p. 8, numbered paras 1, 2, and 3.
7. *a.* Untrue. See p. 9, lines 18-22.   *c.* Untrue. See p. 11, lines 3-12.
   b. Untrue. See p. 9, lines 23-30.
8. Many different stories will be equally "correct". But you could check your work with the Outline on p. 7.
9. *a.* "The old from the new."
   b. Luke says, "He will tear *the new*". Mark and Matthew say that a tear is made in *the old*.
10. See Note **b.** 2 on p. 12.   11. *a.* Matt. 13. 3-8 and 13. 24-30.
12. This is based on p. 9, lines 14-22.   *b.* Matt. 11. 16, 17 and 13. 33.
13. An example is on p. 9, last 7 lines.   *c.* Matt. 15. 11 and 19. 24.

CHAPTER 2. A FARMER AND HIS SEEDS

1. Relies on   believes in   has faith in   commits himself to   trusts
2. See p. 14, lines 31-37.

4. Dug, sowed, fed, mended, repaired, weeded, harvested.
5. See p. 15, lines 4-8.
6. *a.* Untrue. See p. 16, lines 17-21.
   b. True. See p. 16, lines 22-24.
7. See Note **c.** on p. 19.
8. Several verses can be found to support each statement:
   a. 5. 16; 5. 18; 6. 41, 42; 6. 52;
   b. 6. 2; 6. 14, 15; 6. 30;
   c. 6. 60; 6. 64; 6. 66.
9. Two examples were asked for, but there are at least four:
   a leper (Matt. 8. 2 and 3)   Peter's mother-in-law (8. 14)
   "possessed" people (8. 16)   two "possessed" men (8. 28)
10. *a.* Psalm 46.   *b.* Verse 1.
11. See p. 18, lines 4-6.
12. This is based on p. 15, last 5 lines, and p. 16, lines 1-8.
14. This is based on Note **b.** on p. 18 and p. 19.
15. This is based on Note **a.** on p. 18.
16. See p. 19, lines 3-14.

CHAPTER 3.   A FARMER AND HIS HARVEST

1. *Blasphemy* is any dishonour done by man to God. See Mark 2. 7.
   Sorcery is using magic. See Mark 3. 22.
2. Hope   trust   faith.   6. See p. 26, last 4 lines.
3. See p. 22, lines 24-34.   7. See p. 28, lines 6-9.
4. See Note **c.** on p. 28.   8. See p. 26, lines 1-10.
5. See Note **a.** on p. 26.   9. Verse 6b.
10. *a.* The Woman and her Yeast *or* the Children at Play.
    b. The Mustard Seed.
11. See Outline on p. 22.

SPECIAL NOTE A.   THE INTERPRETATION OF THE PARABLES BY THE EARLY CHURCH

1. Application   explanation   sermon.
3. See p. 31, lines 14-19.
4. *a.* See p. 31, line 27.   *b.* See p. 31, lines 30-32.
5. See p. 31, last 8 lines, and p. 32, lines 1-3.
6. See p. 32, lines 26-28.   7. See p. 33, lines 5-14.
8. *a.* 1. Verses 8b and 9;   2. Verses 10-12;   3. Verse 13.
   b. See p. 33, lines 23-37.
9. *a.* The parable is in verses 16-20. Verse 21 is added.
   b. The parable is in verses 31, 32. Verse 33 is added.
   c. The parable is in verses 8, 9. Verse 10 is added.

10. *a.* To tell what kind of weather is coming.
    b. To explain the meaning of something spoken in "tongues of ecstasy".

CHAPTER 4.   A WOMAN AND HER MONEY

1. Prostitutes   thieves   Jews who mix with Gentiles.
2. This is based on p. 38, lines 32-34 .
3. See p. 36, lines 10 and 11.   6. See p. 36, lines 30-37.
4. See p. 40, Note **b.**   7. See p. 37, lines 20-33.
5. See p. 36, lines 24-26.   8. See p. 38, last 4 lines.
9. See p. 40, Note **c.**
10. This is based on p. 37, lines 16-19.
11. See Luke 19. 8.
12. This is based on p. 37, lines 20-33.

CHAPTER 5.   AN EMPLOYER AND HIS WORKMEN

1. This is based on p. 45, line 13 to p. 46, line 14.
2. *a.* This is based on p. 44, lines 4-18.
   b. This is based on p. 44, lines 19-31.
3. There are many pairs of opposites like "superior" and "inferior", e.g.:

   important and unimportant   first and last
   senior and junior   insiders and outsiders
   rich and poor   upper and lower
   good and bad   above and below
4. See p. 43, last line and p. 44, lines 1 and 2.
5. See p. 45, lines 4-7.   7. See p. 44, lines 19-31.
6. See p. 46, Note **b.**   8. See p. 44, lines 16-18.
9. This is based on p. 46, Note **b.**
   Luke 18. 10-14:
   a. The hearers would expect the Pharisee to be "justified" or "acquitted".
   b. The tax-gatherer is "acquitted".
   c. That people who know their need are the ones who can be rescued.
   Matt. 21. 28-31:
   a. The hearers would expect approval to be given to the son who spoke respectfully to his father.
   b. Approval was given to the other son.
   c. That "believing" means *doing* God's will, rather than talking about it.

13. This is based on p. 44, lines 27-31.
14. They may have felt that they were like the men who were engaged late in the day. God gave Gentiles the same Spirit which He gave to the Jews, whose ancestors had been His Chosen People for a long time.

CHAPTER 6.   A FATHER AND HIS SONS
2. This is based on p. 53, Note **d.**
3. This is based on p. 55, lines 5-20.
    a. Irresponsible, careless, etc.   *b.* Loving, generous, etc.
    c. Satisfied, contented, etc.
4. See p. 56, lines 1-6.
5. *a.* See p. 55, line 28 to the end.
    b. The phrase "treat me as one of your hired servants" is missing.
6. *a.* Untrue. See p. 52, last 3 lines and p. 53, lines 1-7.
    b. True. See p. 52, lines 38-40.   *d.* True. See p. 53, lines 6 and 7.
    c. True. See p. 52, lines 35-37.   *e.* Untrue. See p. 53, lines 8-15.
7. See p. 52, last 3 lines and p. 53, lines 1-7.
8. See p. 53, lines 27-32.   9. See p. 56, lines 12-15.
10. *a.* The people of Nineveh. Jonah 3. 5-9.
    b. Jonah. Jonah 4. 1-4.
11. Psalm 103. 8-14 and Ephesians 2. 4-10.
12. *a.* See p. 56, Note **b.**
13. This is based on p. 52, lines 29-31.
16. This is based on p. 55, lines 28-34.

CHAPTER 7.   A HOST AND HIS GUESTS
1. *Taking offence* is being angry because one's feelings have been hurt. *Losing one's temper* is losing control of one's anger.
2. See p. 59, lines 10-12.
3. See p. 59, lines 24-39 and p. 60, lines 1-4.
4. See p. 60, last 2 lines, and p. 61, line 1.
5. See p. 59, lines 17-18 and p. 65, lines 3-6.
6. See p. 65, Note **f.**   8. *a.* Verses 6, 7.
7. See p. 64, lines 1-9.   *b.* Verses 11-14.
9. Its teaching is that only those who are spiritually hungry can accept what God offers.
10. In many ways, e.g.: they were hungry and thirsty, they were willing to accept help.
11. *a.* i. To prepare for the Passover.
        ii. To be cured by the water of the pool.
        iii. To die.
    b. i. The word of God.   ii. The Holy Spirit.
12. See Acts 13. 44-48.

SPECIAL NOTE B.   PARABLES AND ALLEGORIES
1. See p. 67, lines 4-12.
2. *a.* Untrue. See p. 67, lines 26-31.
   b. True. See p. 67, lines 7 and 24.
   c. True. See p. 68, lines 27-30.
   d. Untrue. See p. 69, lines 4-24.
3. See p. 67, lines 15-25.   4. P. 68, lines 9-21.
5. See p. 69, last 11 lines.
6. See p. 68, lines 27-30 and p. 69, lines 27-30.
7. Examples of false teaching which a reader might get are:
   a. That God sleeps, or that God is unwilling to answer prayers.
   b. That people should be forced to become Christians.
   c. That God approves of dishonest practices.
8. *a.* See 2 Sam. 12. 9.
   b. Because it was a story about ordinary life which Nathan told to show David what his life should become.
9. *a.* Because each part of the story gives a separate lesson.
   b. i. God.   iii. Individual Israelites.
        ii. The nation of Israel.
10. This is based on p. 69, line 4 onward.

CHAPTER 8.   TRAVELLERS ON THE ROAD
1. See p. 71, lines 24-26.
2. *a.* Someone who lives nearby.   *b.* A fellow-Jew.
   c. Someone who meets the need of another human being.
3. This is based on p. 76, Note **d.** 1.
   a. See p. 117, line 7 to p. 118, line 15.
4. To live fully and abundantly on this earth.
   To live fully on this earth and after death.
5. *a.* See Luke 10. 33.   *b.* See Luke 10. 34, 35.
6. See p. 72, lines 11-17.
7. See p. 73, lines 35-44 and p. 74, lines 1-6.
8. See p. 74, lines 20-30.
9. See p. 75, Note **a.**
10. See p. 76, Note **b.**
11. This is based on p. 78, Note **f.**
12. *a.* That people who really love God show love to their fellow men also.
    b. That people who love their fellow men are showing love to God also.
13. Many words and phrases describe his behaviour, e.g.:
    Patient   kind   bears all things.
16. *a.* About 200.
    b. Most of them at Nablus, some in Jaffa and other parts of Israel.

127

CHAPTER 9. A FARMER AND HIS TREASURE, AND A TRADER AND HIS BUSINESS

1. See p. 85, Note **c.**
2. *a.* He found a treasure in the ground.
   b. i. Psalm 16. 11.　　　ii. Gal. 5. 22.　　　iii. Acts 5. 41.
3. *a.* See p. 80, last paragraph, and p. 81, lines 1-4.
   b. One difference is referred to on p. 84, Note **a.**
4. *a.* See p. 82, last 7 lines.　　　*b.* See p. 84, lines 1-3.
   c. See p. 84, lines 4-15.
5. See p. 84, Note **b.**
6. *a.* See p. 81, last 5 lines, and p. 82, lines 1-24.
   b. See p. 82, lines 25-31.
7. Matt. 5. 8: Blessedness　　　Rom. 8. 1: Being in Christ Jesus
   Matt. 19. 29: Eternal life　　　Gal. 2. 19: Living to God
   Acts 16. 17: Way of Salvation　　Titus 3. 7: Eternal life
   Rom. 7. 6: The life of the Spirit
8. *a.* In several ways, e.g.:
   In both passages someone had to give up something in order to obtain something even more precious.
   b. In several ways, e.g.:
   In the story in Mark 10. 17-22 the man who could have obtained the precious thing was not willing to pay the cost: in the two parables the farmer and the trader were both willing.
9. This is based on p. 85, Note **c.**
   a. . . . . . the man sold all that he had and bought the field.
   b. . . . . . the fisherman separated the good fish from the bad when his net was full.
10. This is based on p. 81, numbered paragraphs 1 and 3.

CHAPTER 10. A RICH MAN AND HIS DEBTOR

2. See p. 88, lines 6-10.　　　　3. E.g. Pardon.
4. Friendship　sonship　fellowship　worship　leadership
5. See p. 88, lines 3 and 4.　　　7. See p. 87, lines 32-38.
6. See Matt. 18. 25.　　　　　　8. See p. 88, lines 21-25.
9. See p. 88, lines 26-36.
10. *a.* Untrue. See p. 89, lines 27-31.
    b. Untrue. See p. 89, lines 32-38.
    c. Untrue. See p. 93, Note **c.**
11. *a.* See p. 89, lines 10-13.
    b. See Matt. 18. 27 for two results.
12. See Matt. 6. 12.
13. Luke 17. 7-10:　　　　　　Matt. 5. 15:
    a. See p. 92, lines 29 and 30.　*a.* See p. 92, lines 32 and 33.
    b. See Luke 17. 10*b.*　　　　*b.* The whole verse.

14. *a.* See p. 89, lines 32-38.
   b. See p. 89, line 39 to the end, and p. 91, lines 1-10.
   c. See p. 89, lines 32-38.
15. Verses 3, 4; verses 8-12; verse 17.
16. See p. 88, lines 21-25 and p. 91, lines 11-18 and other parts of this chapter.
17. This is based on p. 88, last 7 lines and p. 89, lines 1-13.

SPECIAL NOTE C. JESUS' PARABLES AND
OUR OWN PARABLES, FABLES, ETC.
 1. *a.* See p. 95, lines 28 and 29.
   b. See p. 97, lines 25-27.   *c.* See p. 98, line 14.
   d. See p. 98, last 5 lines, and p. 99, lines 1-3.
 2. Two examples of other meanings are:
   A falsehood.
   A tale which is told or written in order to amuse or interest others: it can be a true story or an invented one.
 3. See p. 95, lines 5-7.   4. See p. 95, lines 30-34.
 5. See p. 98, lines 24-26.   6. See p. 99, lines 16-31.
 7. *a.* See p. 99, last line, and p. 100, lines 1-8.
   b. See p. 100, lines 32-37.
 8. See p. 101, lines 7-21.
 9. *a.* The Empty Petrol Tank for Romans 8. 13.
   b. The Faithful Friend for John 15. 13.
   c. The Rusty Bicycle for Psalm 51. 10.
10. Mark 2. 15:
   a. Eating with people of bad reputation.
   b. Showing that God was in Him, caring about such people and wanting to rescue them.
   Mark 10. 46-52:
   a. Curing blind Bartimaeus.   *b.* See p. 101, lines 13-15.
12. *a.* This is based on p. 97, lines 35-40.

CHAPTER 11. BRIDESMAIDS AND A BRIDEGROOM
 1. This is based on p. 105, lines 20-27.
 2. *a.* Testing   turning-point   judgement-day
 3. See p. 103, last 6 lines, and p. 104, lines 1-18.
 4. See Matt. 25. 6.   5. See p. 106, lines 13-18.
 6. See p. 103, lines 20-23 and p. 106, lines 3-8.
 7. Yona Kanamuzeyi   the bridesmaids who brought extra oil.
 8. See p. 109, Note **e**. 2.
 9. *a.* True. See p. 103, lines 8 and 9.
   b. Untrue. See Matt. 25. 5 and p. 103, lines 11 and 12.
   c. True. See p. 104, lines 9-18.   *d.* Untrue. See p. 109, Note **e**. 2.

10. *b.* See p. 108, lines 14-20.
11. *a.* Several kinds of behaviour, e.g.: praying to God instead of caring for people in need; treating the poor unjustly and cruelly.
    b. Their city would be destroyed. See Isaiah 1. 20.
    c. They are a warning.
15. *b.* See p. 108, lines 1-12.

CHAPTER 12. A HOUSEHOLDER AND HIS SERVANTS

1. *b. Responsibility:*   courage   reliable   trustworthy
   Dependence: lean   baby   weakness
2. *a.* See p. 120, Note **c.**
   b. See p. 114, lines 5-9 of text.
3. See p. 116, lines 33-35.   4. See p. 112, lines 7 and 8.
5. See Matt. 25. 25 and p. 112, lines 11-13.
6. See p. 113, lines 19-27.   7. See p. 113, last 3 lines.
8. *a.* See p. 117, lines 8-15.   *b.* See p. 117, lines 28-36.
   c. See p. 117, line 37 to the end.
9. *a.* See p. 118, lines 33-35.   *b.* Mark 12. 6.
10. See p. 120 and p. 121, Note **f.**
11. *a.* See Luke 12. 20.
    b. See Luke 16, verse 4, or verses 5-7, or verse 8.
    c. See Luke 16, verse 25, or verse 29, or verse 31.
12. *a.* See p. 113, lines 36-41.   *b.* See p. 114, lines 10-13.
    c. In this verse Paul teaches that we are responsible sons of God and must actively use the power He has given us.
13. *a.* See p. 76, Notes **b** and **d.**   *b.* See p. 52, lines 29-31.
    c. There was a danger that she might be treated even more harshly because she kept on bothering the judge.
14. *a.* Several possible reasons, e.g. jealousy, fear. See p. 115 lines 19-21 of text.
19. *a.* See p. 112, lines 7 and 8, and p. 115, lines 2 and 3 of text.

An Alphabetical List of the Parables referred to in this book

Bold type indicates those pages where the parable receives special comment